'An intuition of the particular'

ALSO BY IAN BRINTON
Dickens' Great Expectations, A Reader's Guide (London: Continuum 2007)
Contemporary Poetry: Poets and Poetry since 1990 (Cambridge Contexts in
 Literature; Cambridge: Cambridge University Press, 2009)
A Manner of Utterance, The Poetry of J.H. Prynne (Exeter: Shearsman Books, 2009)
Brontë's Wuthering Heights, A Reader's Guide (London: Continuum 2010);
An Andrew Crozier Reader (Manchester: Carcanet Press, 2012);
Poems of Yves Bonnefoy 1, (Oystercatcher Press, 2013)

ALSO BY PETER HUGHES
The Interior Designer's Late Morning, Many Press 1983
Bar Magenta (with Simon Marsh), Many Press, 1986
Odes on St. Cecilia's Day, Poetical Histories, 1990
The Metro Poems, Many Press, 1992
Psyche in the Gargano, Equipage, 1995
Paul Klee's Diary, Equipage, 1995
Keith Tippet Plays Tonight, Maquette Press, 1999
Blueroads: Selected Poems, Salt Publishing, 2003
Sound Signals Advising of Presence, infernal methods, 2006
Minor Yours, Oystercatcher Press, 2006
Nistanimera, Shearsman Books, 2007
The Sardine Tree, Oystercatcher, 2008
The Summer of Agios Dimitrios, Shearsman, 2009
Behoven, Oystercatcher, 2009
The Pistol Tree Poems (with Simon Marsh), Shearsman, 2011
Interscriptions (with John Hall), Knives Forks And Spoons Press, 2011
Regulation Cascade, Oystercatcher, 2012
Soft Rush, Red Ceilings Press, 2013
Quite Frankly, Like This Press, 2013
Selected Poems, Shearsman, 2013

AS EDITOR
Sea Pie: A Shearsman Anthology of Oystercatcher Poetry, Shearsman 2012

'An intuition of the particular'

some essays
on the poetry
of Peter Hughes

edited by
Ian Brinton

Shearsman Books

First published in the United Kingdom in 2013 by
Shearsman Books Ltd
50 Westons Hill Drive
Emersons Green
BRISTOL
BS16 7DF

Shearsman Books Ltd Registered Office
30–31 St. James Place, Mangotsfield, Bristol BS16 9JB
(this address not for correspondence)

ISBN 978-1-84861-296-9
First Edition

The right of the individual writers to be identified as the authors
of these essays has been asserted by them in accordance with the
Copyrights, Designs and Patents Act of 1988.
All rights reserved.

Copyright in each essay remains with its author, © 2013.
Introduction copyright © Ian Brinton, 2013.

Contents

Introduction by Ian Brinton	9
John Welch: An Interview with Peter Hughes	13
Peter Riley: *The Metro Poems*	24
Derek Slade: Three Poems from *Blueroads*	33
David Kennedy: The International Language of Fish	54
John Hall: ET: The Missing Letters of Peter Hughes' *Behoven*	67
Andrew Bailey: *The Summer of Agios Dimitrios*: Had Me a Blast	84
Simon Marsh: Pulling on the Feathered Leggings	93
Gene Tanta: Why Poetic Collaboration Matters	102
Riccardo Duranti: The Italian Filter	107
Simon Howard: Peter Hughes' Petrarch	117
Nigel Wheale : Riffingly — A Right Read-Through	133
Ian McMillan: Oystercatcher Press	139
John Welch: Publishing Peter Hughes	142

'An intuition…

Introduction:
'a tuning-fork against illusion'

In his Parisian lecture to the 'Association des traducteurs littéraires de France' in 1976 Yves Bonnefoy suggested that we must come to understand the nature of poetry translation as poetry re-begun. And in any new beginning there is a new creation as was recognised by Bernard Dubourg, the translator of both J.H. Prynne and Anthony Barnett, when he addressed the issue of the art of translation for *Grosseteste Review* volume 12 in 1979. Dubourg claimed that to translate is to find yourself a twin, "to light upon a twin to which you can forthwith claim the minority":

> The technique of translation, of which no one can properly define the items, serves to conceal the fact that a good translation contains a greater number of possible senses than the original, being the result of two labours instead of one, and it's for the reader to profit by it.

When Peter Hughes' twenty English versions of the sonnets of Petrarch appeared in October 2012 from Oystercatcher under the title *Regulation Cascade* it came as a delight but no surprise since, after all, here was a poet who had already collaborated with fellow poets, notably John Hall and Simon Marsh: after all, the versions of the Italian fourteenth-century poet are another collaborative effort. In his own contribution to this volume of essays, 'Pulling on the Feathered Leggings', Marsh refers to the ability Hughes has to "blend and transform" and this quality, a translation of one world into another, a metamorphosis in which a moment of Heraclitean movement passes into "the idea of a poem", is perhaps nowhere more clear than in these new versions of Petrarch.

The first poem in the volume presents a thrust of understanding towards the Italian poet's sonnet 34, 'Apollo, s'ancor vive il bel desio', where the god's dashing pursuit of Daphne is merged with another of his roles as patron of poetry. As the fleeing nymph, the Laura / laurel of Petrarch's focus on love, merges into a tree so the fleeting ideas of the invisible become stationary and defined, halted as it were in the lines of a poem:

> I invoke the idea of a poem as
> perpetual enactment of pursuit

> of passion of flight forever turning
> into your damp cavern & formation

With a glance over the shoulder at Keats's "leaf-fringed legend" of "mad pursuit" Peter Hughes calls up his Muse to assist in the act of metamorphosis "as living light changes this appearance" and that which was movement becomes stilled. Clarity dispels darkness, "l'aere disgombra" now "surfaces through you-tube & saliva" and both "night" and "ground" move via the poetic act "through air & all is increasingly clear". In one graceful dance ideas take on palpability and a thought becomes a poem.

Peter Hughes translates Petrarch's Italy into a landscape of the Norfolk coast and sonnet 35, where the early Renaissance poet wanders "Solo e pensoso i piu deserti campi", becomes

> I walk that lonesome road until it ends
> in scabby paddocks rank with thistle
> vacancies of unregarded salt-marsh
> & hissing shingle slopes down to the sea

With the meditative mourning tones of Nathaniel Shilkret and Gene Austin, in the 1927 song 'The Lonesome Road', the style of the African-American folk song measures out the imprisoned distances of Petrarch's "vo mesurando a passi tardi e lenti". This recent Oystercatcher is the first section from Hughes' planned opus of Petrarchan translation and more is to be expected from both Like This Press and Gratton Street Irregular. Thirty more of them, sonnets 67–96, under the title *Soft Rush*, have already appeared in a limited edition from Red Ceilings Press and one of these, 'Erano i capei d'oro a l'aura sparsi', evokes a world where the memory of sensual beauty ensures that the poet's relationship with his lady does not simply dwindle into age and forgetfulness. Hughes' version opens with the tension of what is and what is not:

> a deft breeze slightly lifted surprising
> qualities of fair hair woven with light
> from her eyes extensive swathes of elsewhere
> via memory into now where she is not

That precise use of "deft" has a painter's eye that has captured the briefest of moments opening out into a landscape of the past. A breeze that slightly lifts the hair becomes the door to a wealth, "extensive swathes", belonging once "where she is not" and brought into the "now" along the via / path of memory. The sonnet concludes with a sense of continuity that takes us into the future and the original Italian, with its image of a heart wounded by a bow that has lost its potency, becomes the domesticity of relationship which finds form in the togetherness of a walk through wild weather:

> where weird late sun slants downwards through storm clouds
> out over a desolate valley road
> we'll walk unaccompanied tomorrow

The togetherness of the first person plural in that last line is tinged with a sense of mortality and the isolation of a movement towards death which is always "unaccompanied".

Reviewing *Behoven* for Todd Swift's online magazine *Eyewear* I quoted from George Steiner's 1997 book, *Errata*, a deeply moving collection of autobiographical sketches. Writing about musical criticism Steiner suggested that whilst "talk" enlists "metaphor, simile, analogy" in a more or less impressionistic way, music, coming before language, is a "primal burst out of nothingness": the fall of man can be seen as a withdrawal into the rational explanation involved in verbal expression. Languages appear as registers of separate particularities after the collapse of Babel and Steiner re-created his early years in terms of those very aspects of the particular:

> I grew possessed by an intuition of the particular, of diversities so numerous that no labour of classification and enumeration could exhaust them. Each leaf differed from any other on each differing tree… each blade of grass, each pebble on the lake-shore was, eternally "just so". No repetition of measurement, however closely calibrated, in whatever controlled vacuum it was carried out, could ever be perfectly the same.

A focus upon the particular and an awareness of the unrepeatable nature of the perpetually moving universe are both central to the poetry of Peter Hughes and it is no accident that when interviewed by John Welch he should have talked of the journal he kept which became reduced to "some isolated fragments which seemed to re-enact a mood, the experience of being there, a condensation of language". Early in that interview Hughes talked about his childhood and the "clues" that led him towards poetry. For instance being taken to the libraries every week he remembered choosing non-fiction books about "Space, dinosaurs, rocks" and recalled a Primary

School teacher who would entertain his pupils by bringing in "moles that had been run over, bits of pheasant that had tarmac sticking to them" and who would play his pupils lots of music: "all this to generate poetry." These autobiographical fragments of memory inevitably call to mind the conversations that Basil Bunting had with Jonathan Williams, *Descant on Rawthey's Madrigal* (gnomon press 1968), in which the Northumbrian poet recalled his father's close concern with histology:

> There was in those days an animal shop in Newcastle and he had an arrangement: when an animal died he would be called at once and go and remove the particular glands he wanted to examine before anything else was done. So he managed to have lions, tigers, leopards, monkeys, all sorts of things on his list besides the small animals he could buy for the purpose. The house was sometimes full of lizards that had escaped from their box in the cellar.

It was this background that prompted Bunting to tell Peter Makin in December 1984 that "Suckling poets should be fed on Darwin till they are filled with the elegance of things seen or heard or touched". In a similar manner the young Hughes tramped through the Berkshire Downs where "there was no distinction between the poetry and place or poetry and history" and it is this palpability, this sense of exactness, an understanding of how language evokes place that prompts so many of his poems to be what Derek Slade quotes as "events in language rather than vehicles for sentiment or anecdote."

However, the poetry of Peter Hughes is much more than just a world of particularity and he has, time and again, threading through his work the ability to condense the universal into the field of local habitation and name. Confronting the inescapable nature of mutability he recognises both the impassioned cry of Lycaon, clutching the knees of the nemesis Achilles in Book XXI of the *Iliad*, and the inevitability of the Greek hero's response. As he puts it in the opening lines of the second movement of his 'Quintet for St. Cecilia's Day':

> I don't think any significant distances have been covered
> since the landlord traipsed by with servant and bandy gait
> a couple of days or weeks or centuries ago.

This oeuvre of poems provides the reader with, in the words of Steiner, "a tuning-fork against illusion."

An Interview with Peter Hughes

This interview was conducted by John Welch at Peter and his partner Lynn's home in Hunstanton on the north Norfolk coast in 2009, and concluded by email.

JW: *How did it start?*

PH: My first encounter with poetry—I suppose it was at school. My parents took me to two libraries every week, the one in the village and the one in Cowley. But most of the books I chose would be non-fiction. Space, dinosaurs, rocks. Or endless series of *Biggles* and *Just William* stories. Then I had a teacher at primary school called Michael Strangeways who was quite young—it was probably his first teaching job. I can remember when I started at that school in 1961 there were various old teachers, reading from ancient *Janet and John* books and stories about gormless rabbits. I can't remember learning to read, but it was strange having these very old-fashioned teaching methods where an old person stood in front of the class and talked to you and if anything bad happened would say "I have a solution for everything. Philip spat at Linda in the playground and he will therefore sit behind the piano and fill this jam jar with spit and won't come out until it's full." Contrasting with all that was this young teacher, Michael Strangeways, who would pile groups of us into a minibus and drop us off at various locations in the Berkshire Downs. It must have been entirely illegal, I would think. He would make little clues as to where each group had to go and they would be in rhyming quatrains or written in runes—he was a Tolkien aficionado, and had read us *The Hobbit*. So we'd peer at these scraps of verse and try to relate them to the map and what we could see around us. Or he would bring in moles that had been run over, bits of pheasant that had tarmac sticking to them, and play us lots of music—all this to generate poetry. We didn't do any Maths for the whole year in his class that I can remember. But I was lucky enough to be in his class twice, with another teacher in between. I think the first time I became aware of poetry was through him. Poetry, I mean, that seemed worth attending to—as opposed to nursery rhymes or fey effusions about birds being gleeful.

JW: *So you first encountered poetry through these "clues"?*

PH: Yes . . .and through writing poetry and doing drawing and painting in response to music, and through going out along the River Cherwell, or on these strange excursions to the Berkshire Downs where landscape and history, the history of landscape and history of language, were all interwoven. He would take some of us off on a Saturday, again through the Berkshire Downs, past Wayland's Smithy and White Horse Hill. There was no distinction between the poetry and place or poetry and history. To him it seemed a natural way of relating to the world. I don't know if he was a poet. All that was extremely important to me, the fact that an adult could be passionate about it.

JW: *It sounds remarkable. And as you say he couldn't work like that nowadays.*

PH: No! The next thing I can remember in terms of poetry, at school, was reading Hardy in class, *Far From the Madding Crowd*, and having an almost visceral reaction to bits of writing. There's a bit where Boldwood is walking across a field one morning, preoccupied, with his veins bulging, his jealousy working overtime. He looks down at his boots covered with colour from the buttercups. They had become bronzed with this effect. It's one of those moments where you see something in writing for the first time, something that you yourself have experienced, and it somehow seems wrong, it seems improbable, intrusive almost, that somebody else has noticed that. One of those moments which seem to validate your own experience as being worthy of being written. At the same time, of course, what you read is changing what you see. But I can't remember quite how I got involved in writing outside of school. I wrote songs—I did a lot of music as a teenager and wrote songs for little bands I was in. Then I had a year out of school and worked as a milkman, then hiring out boats, then working as a stagehand. I got to know Shaw's *St. Joan* very well! I went to art college for a year, left and went down to the Scillies.

JW: *Why did you leave after a year?*

PH: I wasn't getting much out of it and I went down to the Scillies in the Easter holidays, fell in love with the place and wanted to go back. I ended up spending a year, doing some farm work, and a lot of reading. I kept a sort of journal and ended up throwing everything away except for some isolated fragments which seemed to re-enact a mood, the experience of being there, a condensation of language. That led naturally into trying to link some of these pieces into free-standing poems. The following Autumn I went off to Cambridge to do a degree in English. I realised that was what I wanted to do. That was at the "Tech", the Cambridge College of Arts and Technology. John James was teaching there, and Nigel Wheale.

JW: *Were you actually taught by them?*

PH: I was taught briefly by Nigel. He did a seminar on Shakespeare's late romances. He'd only just got there. I don't think John ever taught me. But I started reading his poetry. And Nigel would lend me books of American poetry.

JW: *What year would that have been?*

PH: I was there from 1978 to 1981. There was quite a lot going on, because there was the Cambridge Poetry Festival. There was a big international presence. I became more aware of European poetry through the festival. But it was coming to an end. Later, in 1991 or 1992, it would be "replaced" by the CCCP.

JW: *For a time there was a fringe festival as well. I remember reading with Nigel Wheale at the fringe.*

PH: Yes, I did too. My first reading. It was terrifying. In fact it was Nigel who asked me if I sent poetry off anywhere. I hadn't, so he gave me three or four suggestions, one of which was The Many Press. I hadn't sent anything off to any magazines at that point. I'd ended up in Brighton, after I'd graduated. I sent you those poems from there, I think. I went to a party, stayed the night and ended up staying several months and getting a job delivering parcels. I arranged to do a part-time M.A. at Sussex, with Andrew Crozier. But I unexpectedly got a grant to do a full-time course. At that time, the only post-graduate course in modern poetry was at Stirling, so that's where I went.

JW: *I remember getting those poems, and they struck me as very accomplished.*

PH: I was very startled to have them accepted. It was a great moment!

JW: *So you'd been at Cambridge, and had been in touch with two people* *who were connected to what had been going on in Cambridge poetry from the mid-1960s. John James in particular was in at the beginning it. So was there a growing awareness on your part of all of that?*

PH: I don't think I became really aware of that till after I'd left, strangely enough. When I went to Italy in 1983 to work I started buying books from Peter Riley's list, and it was really then that I started to explore, firstly through John James' work, some of the other things that were going on. There was the anthology *A Various Art* which came out, in 1987, edited by Andrew Crozier and Tim Longville. Then work from the small presses, including yours.

JW: *So you were "doing the TEFL", teaching English as a Foreign Language, for many a rite of passage at the outset of a career, and you actually stayed in Italy for quite a long time?*

PH: I went to L'Aquila in September 1983, and then moved to Rome after about six months. I wasn't paying very much attention at that time to other people's writing and I wasn't thinking very much about stylistic issues, I was just aiming to respond to being in Italy. I was writing *The Metro Poems*, which hovered around a sonnet shape, but were quirkier than my earlier things. Then *Bar Magenta*, with Simon Marsh. I moved back from Rome to Cambridge just in time for the first Cambridge Conference of Contemporary Poetry, at which I'd been invited to read. In the early '90s. I think that was Nigel's doing too.

JW: *Yes,* The Metro Poems *had more of a sense of random elements brought together. A combination of the rural and the urban—Rome is quite a small city of course—and also a strong presence of the sea, and an interest in the night sky.*

PH: Yes, sea and night sky. When I was a kid, my parents were always taking us off camping, several times a year. We got close to the sea and night sky every few weeks—sometimes a bit too close. I remember hanging on to guy-ropes, as the tent rose into Welsh downpour, like a malignant kite. When I was in Scotland, and then the following year in the even colder environment of Abruzzo, the night skies were quite stunning, with very little light pollution up in the Apennines. I've always found—and this may go back to Hardy as well—that juxtaposition of the very small and transient with the biggest possible, and the way those things move against each other, stirring. I look back at some poems of mine and think "that's a religious poem for atheists". Billowing awe and wonder on a cosmic scale held down by a few plastic tent-pegs. Reminds me of Doug Oliver's comment in 'An Island that is all the World': "What does it mean to talk of spirituality in poetry when no religious belief lies behind the enquiry?"

JW: *Was Rome important in other ways, as the "eternal city". A lot of your references are quite gamy, corruption and other forms of louche behaviour. Your Italian did get very good?*

PH: Yes. I ended up doing a lot of translation work. But I was there for several years so it did have a chance to improve. I had some exciting times. Romantically complex years, to say the least. I think I'd always been fairly withdrawn, but being in a new environment in a new country, and behaving in a new language, I found very liberating. I was brought up as a Roman Catholic, not very strictly, and spent my teenage years despising the Catholic church and everything about it. I wouldn't have been able to look at religious painting or listen to religious music with any patience. Another thing that happened in Rome was that I fell in love with baroque art. And the gaminess of Caravaggio was part of that.

JW: *And also Saint Cecilia? You have a number of poems addressed to her.*

PH: The embracing of all that imagery in a way that was freed from what were for me previously repressive religious experiences was very exciting. I became obsessive about tracking down paintings and sculptures, doing the rounds of Rome and elsewhere. I kept my teaching down to a couple of days each week and would go off on endless train journeys all over Italy. The St. Cecilia theme brought together all the arts, of course. And Frank O'Hara somewhere said we weren't allowed to write about her any more—so I did.

JW: *I stayed with you in Rome on two occasions—I have written about it in my prose book* Dreaming Arrival. *For me it was a sense of continuity that struck me, where the emperor appears to metamorphose into the pope, and the vestal virgins become nuns. I remember you taking me to a church once where women go who are trying to get pregnant, and the goddess Juno has turned into…*

PH: The 'Madonna of Childbirth' in Sant' Agostino. Yes I can see the statue, by Sansovino. And I can see the local deities and nature spirits turning into the pantheon of saints. There's a good Caravaggio there too—the grubby soles of peasant feet foregrounded. It was the opportunity to spend some years walking not just past but through those spaces, by Borromini for example, the statues of Bernini, the paintings of Caravaggio and all the rest … I still feel it's part of my "home". I did a piece recently called 'Italia' which had thirty sections, one for each of the Italian provinces. Italy is still there in my writing, partly because of my ongoing collaboration with Simon Marsh. Today I'm expecting *The Pistol Tree Poems* Number 58. There will be 106 in total, simply because the first one I did and sent to Simon happened to have fifty three lines. He wrote back a mirror image of it, with fifty three lines. So for number three I did fifty two lines and he echoed that. We're half way through in terms of the number of poems but in terms of the mass of writing we're getting quite near the end.

JW: *So there's an element of process here, using arbitrary procedures. But also an element of improvisation? As musicians might improvise?*

PH: Yes, very much so. Picking up elements from previous poems which may lie fallow for half a dozen sections or more, and then re-emerge like a thread to be woven back into the sequence. And introducing new material which may initially seem completely at odds with what's gone before. Contrasts in tone, register. Embracing the "unpoetic". We did use to play music together when we shared a house as students in Cambridge. We both played guitar. Simon still plays every week and plays with bands. I'm not sure how that's going now because he's bought a house and moved out of Milan, but he still works in Milan four days a week.

JW: *And is music still important to you?*

PH: I got to a point, back in England when I was deputy head teacher in a primary school in Cambridge, when I was still trying to do music (mainly saxophone by this point) and painting and writing and I ended up doing pretty much nothing in a satisfying way. So I stopped writing for a couple of years, stopped the music apart from joining an informal group of jazz musicians who met a couple of times a month, and concentrated on painting. I did Cambridge Open Studios for several years, with four weekends a year which I did in Peter Riley's bookshop. It wasn't really until May 2006 that I started writing again in a very purposeful way. By then I knew that I had to leave teaching, and school management. The first *Pistol Tree* poems were about that time and I started writing the poems that went into *Nistanimera*, which was published by Shearsman. Salt had done *Blue Roads*, a sort of selected poems up to that point, and it was time to start again.

JW: *So improvisatory techniques, which you've evoked for instance in 'Keith Tippett Plays Tonight', which came out as a pamphlet in 1999, were an influence?*

PH: I've often found that the writing I've enjoyed most has been written at some speed, sometimes while listening to music, though I don't tend to do that so much now. It still interests me as a way of informing writing. For example I did a long, over 70-page, poem called 'Berlioz' not so long ago which again was about getting back to writing and putting the instruments up in the attic, the saxophone as well as the guitar. It was interesting thinking about writing using the composer's career and the different ways that he'd composed and performed, as a sort of metaphor. But it's a kind of narrative poem too. (Something else you're not allowed to do.)

JW: *Simon Marsh stayed in Italy, but you decided to come back…*

PH: My first wife and I came back when our son Tom was about two. I was more reluctant than my wife. I certainly wanted to stop doing TEFL. In a way I had almost stopped when Tom was born. I'd cut down my teaching to about two days a week. I worked for the Italian National Bank, for a helicopter factory down in Frosinone and I worked for the Italian army at one point. The Italian contribution to the war in Afghanistan about the time of the Russian withdrawal was to train the Pakistani army to clear minefields. And there was an amazing variety of mines left behind, ranging from 1940s wooden Czechoslovakian box mines to the very high-tech fibreglass things that were dropped from the air, and primed by contact with the ground when a fragile glass phial of acid would start eating away a thin metal wire. They would teach me about mines in Italian in the morning, we'd go to the Officers' Mess for lunch. After lunch I would teach it to them back in English. All that was quite surreal. A long table covered in coffee cups and bits of grenades. I'd cut down the teaching to spend more time with Tom, so I started doing more translation work. I wish we'd had the internet then. I spent hours delivering translations around Rome.

JW: *Were there any Italian poets that meant a lot to you, or that you had had contact with?*

PH: I read the highlights of Italian literature in the years I was there. The person that ended up meaning most to me was Pasolini. I still find it fascinating the way that he brings together the personal, political, local, cosmic, dialect and formal resources. He writes about very ordinary, untouristy aspects of Rome and Italy, but using quite formal means sometimes, Dante's *terza rima* for example. So you get this interesting juxtaposition: classical, very resonant form and earthy accounts of poverty and corruption, which I find compelling. And his prose was great. Regular thorns in the sides of a corrupt, sanctimonious establishment. Nothing has changed there. Berlusconi's party appears to be the product of *mafiosi* think-tanks.

I went to Italy knowing (in translation) some Dante, then some of the earlier 20th century poets. Ungaretti, Montale, Quasimodo, Sereni, Fortini. Once there, I became interested in more recent work. Andrea Zanzotto seemed to be in a category all of his own, though he was sometimes linked to a ghostly school of Neo-Hermeticism. Amelia Rosselli, who lived in Rome, is a significant voice. Then the more self-consciously avant-garde writers—Giuliani, Sanguineti, Balestrini, Porta. But this was a generation born in the 1930s. With the internet, it's now possible to be much more aware of contemporary Italian poetry through sites such as Absolute Poetry, GAMMM and Nazione Indiana. Linh Dinh has translated some of that work recently. Gherardo Bortolotti, Marco Giovenale and Michelle Zaffarano, for example. So, funnily enough, I'm more in touch with it now than I was then.

JW: *So you're back in England. You stayed in teaching?*

PH: I worked in three different schools in and around Cambridge—five years in each. The damage done to teaching and learning in the primary phase by successive governments since the 1960s is extraordinary. I wasn't very good at implementing certain government initiatives, which led to a bit of tension now and again. So I'm glad to be out of it. Lynn and I celebrated by spending seven weeks in Greece in September and October 2007. Kelvin and Melanie Corcoran kindly lent us their house. The Shearsman book *The Summer of Agios Dimitrios* was written there, in the Mani.

JW: *The next thing of yours that the Many Press published after* The Interior Designer's Late Morning *was* Bar Magenta *which had poems by you and by Simon Marsh, though these were not collaborations in the sense you were describing just now. But you've been doing a lot of collaborative work recently?*

PH: Yes, my poems in *Bar Magenta* were written when I was living in the Veneto. I lived in Vicenza for two years. Again, I took on just enough work to get by so as to leave room for exploring the north of Italy. Train connections were good so I could be in Verona or Padua in 20 minutes. I spent a lot of time in Venice. It was a wonderful opportunity to get to know the north.

Collaboration is important to me. I'm currently involved in a project with Carol Watts called 'Fretworks'. The sequence is evolving, as it should, in ways which couldn't be anticipated at the outset. Last year I worked with John Hall on a sequence of pictures and texts called *Interscriptions*. John is very experienced at working with text in a visual way, to create textual pictures. I wasn't, so it was a privilege to work with him on that. The collaboration with Simon is my most substantial collaborative undertaking though. We've been very lucky to have the hospitality of Peter Philpott's *Great Works* site. The poems have been appearing there since May 2006.

JW: *You referred earlier to your painting. When did you start painting?*

PH: I don't know. I can't remember not painting. I do remember having to change schools when I was 16 because they wouldn't let me do Art A-level. It wasn't academic enough. They tried to make me do Economics instead. So I left. There's often a strong graphic element to my painting—not necessarily drawn lines, often *sgraffito* marks which expose the underpainting. I usually start in acrylic, to get colour and strong texture in quickly, then oil on top. I like cutting back through this in forms suggestive of text or musical notation—though they are usually neither. I've always been fascinated by the way the arts echo through each other. At the moment I'm working on a group of pictures which incorporate text more explicitly, for an exhibition in September.

JW: *In 1995 Equipage published* Paul Klee's Diary. *His work means a lot to you?*

PH: Yes. His dedication to art was exemplary—as a painter, a poet and a musician. I don't tire of his work. Klee, Miró and Kandinsky were my three favourite painters. I suppose now the very idea of using paint to produce paintings seems to many an antiquated way of making art. But for me it's still compelling. Klee's range is very great. His art is extremely inclusive.

JW: *How did you go about excavating these poems from his journals?*

PH: I came to inhabit those journals as one does a favourite novel, often re-read. Then I made many of the episodes chime with similar ones in my life, which then provided some of the detail. So much of the writing ends up having nothing to do with Klee in a literal way. But I hope I was respectful to the spirit of his journals. My procedures were not very purist. They never are.

JW: *How do you situate yourself with regard to current tendencies on the British and American poetry scene? There's that not always clearly-defined but nevertheless quite powerful them-and-us sense, with its attendant paranoias—"mainstream" and "experimental" or "avant-garde".*

PH: I sometimes get the impression that the poets who interest me most are regarded with suspicion by extremists on both sides. How would you situate Kelvin Corcoran, Andrew Crozier, Roy Fisher, Michael Haslam, Randolph Healy, John James, Denise Riley, Peter Riley, Maurice Scully or yourself? (And I'm sorry there's only one woman in that particular list). Well, like them, I tend to write in standard English sentences. But I am not interested in a poem which seems entirely envisaged from the outset—in which there is nothing unexpected. The kind of poem which knows where it's going and concludes by patting itself on the head for getting there. I'm attracted to clashes and jumbles of the felt, the thought, the multi-voiced and dissonant. Some poetry which is considered "innovative" is actually quite conservative in that it inhabits a fixed range of ideological and aesthetic conventions. I'm not interested in writing within a convention. And a lot of innovative poetry is still prim. It is suspicious of humour, sex and the intoxicated. I would like to ship in more of those things, from outlying districts if need be. Also, I don't feel particularly "British". Maybe because my mother is Irish. Maybe because I feel more at home in a European context.

JW: *When we were having dinner with Anthony Mellors recently you did describe very interestingly your fantasy of a sort of "affectless" poem!*

That was just a parody of a certain kind of Creative Writing Class outcome. A poem designed by a committee. Bits of discourse snipped from the media, instruction manuals, political speeches, songs, adverts etc taped together—with any authorial or dramatic voices strictly suppressed. So it would be an "objective" reflection of the world. It wouldn't really. It would just be faulty reception on a second-hand radio.

JW: *What about the Oystercatcher project?*

PH: When I got back to writing I wanted to get something "out there" quickly, so I published *The Sardine Tree*, my sequence based on Miró. I hadn't exactly planned to run a small press. I sent that pamphlet to several people, including John Hall. He told me about his own Miró poem—and that ended up being the next Oystercatcher. Then it kept going. I invited various poets to send work. One of the first was Andrew Crozier, but he was already too ill. A couple of people didn't respond at all. But most responded with warmth, enthusiasm and generosity. I'm pleased to have poets who have been writing since the 1960s as well as those who are relative newcomers. The Oystercatchers of Rufo Quintavalle and Alistair Noon, for example, are their first books. This is certainly not the case with Peter Riley or John Welch. Rufo lives in Paris, Alistair in Berlin. Lisa Samuels is an American in New Zealand. I like the fact that not all the books come out of that manic vortex of cutting-edge art practices which is Hunstanton.

The Metro Poems

Peter Riley

I. Ruins

Looking at *The Metro Poems*[1] again after twenty years I see them as a modern version of 'The Ruins of Rome'. This was a popular 16th Century poem, a set of sonnets, originally *Les Antiquités de Rome* by Joachim du Bellay (1588) translated by Edmund Spenser as *The Ruines of Rome by Bellay*, in *Complaints*, 1591. There is also *The Ruins of Rome* by John Dyer, 1737, a long blank verse poem which is not related. The theme of all these is a melancholy apprehension of how the greatest civilisation the world had known fell to be a collection of ruins. This is generally attributed to a decadence marked by luxuriance ("leisure" in Spenser) and inner conflict. Dyer's is a pedestrian catalogue of ruins with interspersed sentiments, but du Bellay/Spenser speaks only generally of this decay, and is in the end optimistic of a rebirth in modernism and in poetry itself.

I don't propose any deliberate tracking by Peter Hughes of these ancient texts nor even a submerged memory.[2] *The Metro Poems* is a set of short poems whose titles are those of stations on the Rome Metro as it was at the time when he lived there (near the Anagnina Metro terminus) and I think travelled on the Metro most days to work. These names occur in the actual sequence of the stations from north to south (which for him means going home as far as the 22nd poem, but thereafter on a branch line). (Two stations near the end seem to be in reverse order). But the connection between the titles and the poems is unstable, sometimes not apparent at all, and never much more than casual. *Ottaviano* for instance, the title of the first poem, is not at the seaside, in fact it is the nearest station to St Peter's and the Vatican, but we get a shore scene involving gannets, seaweed, bivalves, tides, even whales. I think it's unlikely that these derive from ornamental details of baroque sculpture or that they are satirical

---

[1] First published by The Many Press (John Welch) 1992. Reprinted in *Blueroads* (Cambridge: Salt Publishing 2003) without revision but with three uncorrected errors in lineation.

[2] I did for a moment, when I noticed that Spenser/Bellay consists of 32 sonnets and *The Metro Poems* of 32 poems, also that the first line of the first poem in Spenser ends with "ashie cinders" ("poudreuse cendre") and of *Ottaviano*, the first Metro poem, "tumbly pumice". But there is nothing else in the set to encourage such a connection, and these phenomena must be considered coincidental, abhorrent as such an idea is to some schools of poetry.

references to the Pope. Many more poems have settings which clearly have nothing to do with the place named in the title, often a domestic interior. Nor is there any sequentiality to the poems that I can see, beyond that of their titles, any sense of development to a conclusion through the book, though the poems clearly belong together. Half of them have fourteen lines and there is a sonnet-like movement to many of them, particularly a concluding gestural summation which reminds me of the final couplet of the "English" sonnet form. But I get the impression that the purpose of the Metro structure was quantitative: a demand which the poet set himself to write a substantial number of poems of more-or-less the same kind, and indeed compared with earlier work these poems show a venture to a new threshold, the realisation of a fecundity and tension which made this the first of his writings to command attention. It set in motion a career which is still linked to it.

What I mean by a sense of the ruins of Rome is that the substance of the poems, which is insistently diurnal, stuffed with imagery of the paraphernalia of modernity from bloater pot tops to Smokey Robinson and the Miracles, pursues its own course through the book *under the signs of* the ancient city. These signs represent civic continuity, order, and antiquity, and the living of a current life runs beneath them by its own initiative, like a train in a tunnel under the city, from time to time acknowledging the upper world with or without irony. In the poems the orderly and idealistic sense gained by the succession of important names is undermined by invocation of the actualities of living there, as if that is the more real Rome—this mess, frustrating or delightful as it may be, is what the capital of the world now is as experienced.

The Rome Metro was not constructed to get tourists to their destinations but to get workers to and from the suburbs. We do get titles such as Colosseo, Circo Massimo, Piramide, Arco di Travertino, also S. Giovanni (in Latero) and Vittorio (Emanuele) but even when the titles are Marconi, Cinecittà or Termini they still contribute to an ensemble of Italian (close to Latin) names which delineate the fixed and interlocked presence of the civic entity and its past, under which and largely concealed from which the individual spirit quite happily and relentlessly pursues its course. There is no sense of a resented presiding authority, perhaps more often an exhilaration at threading the modern catacombs of such a venerable place, a privilege, but essentially not bound to it, not dictated to by it. Rather the self pays acknowledgement as necessary, mocks, or bows politely to the statues and inscriptions. (As I remember it, Rome

Metro architecture uses travertine a great deal and many station names are carved in it. The stone itself refers to ancient Rome: the Colosseum is built of it.)

Ottoviano and poems like it operate a sheer and deliberate disconnection from their titles, and a lot of the others transgress them. Yet *Flaminio* is an in-train scene inhabited by "magnanimous aunts" and their sewing, which merges with the witches' scene in *Macbeth*, and *S. Giovanni* ends as a poem about frescoes. A number of poems acknowledge the actual Metro station only at the end of the poem following excursions wildly elsewhere, with a sense of agreeing to a titular demand hitherto ignored, which is a factor of the poetical shaping which is one of Hughes' notable skills, the turn to elsewhere at the end. This is liable to be an emergence from underground[3] at a worthy name which is found to be attached to a particularly dull or even squalid bit of the city ("Pebbles rest on the Metro's leaking roof"). The title *Vittorio* which whether historical or not signifies "victory" and thus the entire structure, elicits after two lines "Night smells of decaying courgettes", dragging it mercilessly down to an untidy market. A poem such as *Porta Furba* treats its title as fortuitous and reinforces this with further fortuities, particularly the sudden and inexplicable presence of Saint Raymund, supine, "carted past like a paralytic half-scrum". There were several saints of this name, none of whom played rugby. The poem is dedicated to Frank O'Hara. Fortuity is, I believe, an important part of Hughes' poetical technique, allowing forms of escape from over-weight signification or constrictive singularity, opening the lines to the multitudinous lives of the city and all their clutter. Fortuity becomes an offered affection. In *Numidio Quadrato*—

> the Roman ruins of Tuscolo
> get back into their cars, rewrap buns
> and offspring squealing onto the Frascati road.

Here the ruins of Rome are the modern population, returning from a trip to the nearby hills, a condition from which the self is not excepted, for a few lines later "we coast back to Frascati" like the rest and the traces of British mud on our wheels don't distinguish us. Everyone has by a poetical sleight-of-hand turned into the ruins they came here to see: the transition from the first line to the second is a swift and unemphatic move creating a metaphor out of two juxtaposed literal conditions, which is typical of this poetry's vigorous or even reckless leaping movement through different

---

[3] Not all of the Rome Metro is underground, but let's not worry about that.

perceptual modes or scenes. The inevitable sense of fortuity attached to this kind of excursion ("The dog mooches about the amphitheatre as I pose on the empty stage…") is held and dignified by a rhyme across the whole poem: "Ethelred" appears inexplicably in the second line, and at the ending we sit in Frascati "wondering why it's twinned with Maidenhead." This witty, energetic and slightly disdainful scenario is typical of much of his work.

Set, therefore, against the constant dignity of the titles there is a sense of a modern condition of cluttered squalor, distraction in a profusion of unavoidable detail, personally owned, and characterised by intermittent senses of loss or disorientation, comfort of sexual affection, crowdedness, and a welter of other things including "leisure and inner conflict", expressed as a verbal heterophony. And all of this is both "under" the Metro names and out there in the open air beyond the stations, an area which is sometimes entered as a relief ("…get out of the Underground and take a proper train Through the moving grasses of Etruria…") and sometimes recognised as a threat ("Fascist graffiti caress Fascist walls"). A realism drawn out of all these conflicting elements is confronted periodically with a bid for sublimity in the working of the poem itself, mainly in conclusions which draw perception upwards towards the celestial (clear or clouded) and move the metrics towards the ancestral. These turns, often last-minute, are perhaps the most important sign that the writing's ethos is not in the end bathetic.

II. The Last-Minute Turn

When it is understood that the body of the poem normally holds a welter of strong verbal movement full of abrupt transitions, outlandish similes and sometimes almost surreal figures, all intermixed with notation of the authentically real in its most inescapably paradoxical guise, the shaping of the poem becomes important. For this inner substance could be extended indefinitely or could peter out in a series of small episodes, scenes, events, wishes etc. without consequence. Indeed when you read through the book consecutively the insistent liveliness can itself become tiring.[4] It is the shaping of the poem in among all this which completes the picture and rescues the material from an engaging but boundless continuity. The confidence of the movement through the poem is what guarantees this, but it is especially clear in endings, of which a selection follows. These are

---

[4] Tiring: a term used in old-fashioned wine journalism for a wine high in alcohol.

all unexpected turns, generally a release at the last moment into a larger sense of being and a longer past which is a firmer possession than civic titles. Five examples—

Lepanto: An edgeland kind of scene with allotments, rusty tractor etc., which turns into the exterior of the Metro station and remains there but is jolted upwards into the last word—

> It was already getting headlight dusk
> When the station bats flicked across Venus.

Furio Camillo: Conversely, a calm domestic poem of night, crickets, she, stars, turns at the end to a further human range, by listening *outside* the house—

> Sleepless, a neighbour
> is murmuring to some god or child.

Subaugusta: A friendly, perky poem "for Saint Cecilia's Day" replete with alcohol and guitar strings allows itself to pass into the next day with a direct quote of the apocalyptic last line of Dryden's 1687 Song, typically taken at a run—

> …trampolines of song that launch us
> On whippy parabolas to crunchy hangover
> Breakfast and music shall untune the sky.

Arco di Travertino: A quite disturbing poem already involved in large-scale imagery of interior conflict and a conversational impasse about death is brought to an end and resolved by a dramatic exit strategy--
> She flicks the light switch but nothing happens.
> I replace the bulb but night keeps falling.

Marconi: The poem with the Fascist graffiti, passing through sparse imagery of waste ground ("waist-high grasses dribbling seed") which repeats itself, finally concedes—

> We are never going to see the light
> threshed tonight in the courtyards of the stars.

All these poems had in a sense already ended prior to these endings, and the further extensions are like envoys. They are all more-or-less unexpected turns which may consummate or negate the questions raised in the poem, but above all they are a withdrawal from the earthly parameters of the poem's vision, turning the attention upwards, sight trained beyond the walls, in what by the reminder of further time and further space must, I think, have a sense of the gentle notification of death—death as a brightening or a darkening but in any event an opening.

There are many other poem-endings entirely without these bids for sublimity, indeed they may be bathetic or denying or just staying inside the earthly question, but nevertheless marked by ancestral rhythms like these. The poems are normally brought to a gentle and firm stand-still a little later than they needed to be for the sake of their evident purpose. And none of this seems heavy or forced, but done with a flourish of virtuosity; the musician supplies a coda, gratis, which acknowledges his own skill, transgressing the terms of employment. Indeed transgression is a constant feature of his style, liable to arrest us at any moment. Earlier in the poem *Lepanto*

>   Sons of old friends pedal mopeds uphill
>   Past allotments…

which is another kind of turn, and we are taken by surprise in a gesture of pact with the human scene, a sense of succeeding generations to which all the individuation bows. The mopeds' shared failure to cope with hills becomes an acknowledgement of a common lasting condition. We get so much *more* than we are entitled to expect.

III. Three Poems

VITTORIO
Stickiness between the fingers of August,
a crunching underfoot in the dark,
the cracking of plastic, wood or shell.
Night smells of decaying courgettes
and dregs from the Castelli,
    fleeting as spit on the tide.

Between the train's weight and the rails,
the inaudible fragmentation

of the heart's friable stone
dusts the sleepers under Vittorio.

This is an instance of the title springing up at the last moment, with the effect of a concession, agreeing to expectation, the last word thrown down like a trump card. But it also shows how unyielding some of the poems can remain in spite of his general fondness for pointed clarity. The poem occupies two distinct places but is quite indirect or evasive in identifying or describing. These are glimpses, and we are left with questions which we're not sure are necessary. There are three appearances of decaying courgettes in the book, all at night. Castelli is a wine-growing region south-east of Rome. The seas around Italy do not have tides. There are uncertainties about the first scene which remain whatever we do. But the cracking of friable substance under the foot walking at night gains a direct echo in the "inaudible fragmentation of the heart's friable stone", which I wouldn't want to reduce by explanation. And all this crunching and breaking-up finally "dusts the sleepers" which I was immediately inclined to take as something like a night-shelter under the station, though wooden sleepers are of course more likely. And the remaining question is, is a stone heart a desirable possession, however friable?—I would have thought not. The heart-event also, then, is an uncertainty, in fact a major one. If we seek resolution, perhaps unwisely, we have only the last word to turn to. We are led to think of "victory" as presiding over all this from start to finish, perhaps in spite of everything in it.

FERMI
It is of no consequence
that wherever a bus-stop sign
is wrenched out of the path
and chucked over a hedge

some priest with new sandals
horny toe-nails and a gold tooth
climbs the gate, wades the wet grass
and waits for the 47.

This is a plain-speaking account which is rare in the book for a whole poem, though there are poem sections like this. It is of course innocently non-committal but hints here and there elsewhere in the book (e.g. in *Termini* a copy of *Catholicism Today* found in a storeroom alongside "dusty unpaired shoes", and see the next poem I quote) might suggest the author's feelings about priests, with which, and nuns, Rome has been described [citation needed] as "infested" worse even than Belfast. Certainly this priest is not an image of dignity and authority. But it is not a problematic or ambivalent poem, and its banner heading of "no consequence" identifies the fortuity at the heart of the scene. I don't know why the station is called *Fermi*, but Peter must know that it is a form of *fermare*: to stop, stay. There are these halts, and you chuck them over the hedge, but they climb back over the gate in the form of a priest.

> REPUBBLICA
> An uneasy combination of Sardinian wine
> and Venus has risen over the petrol station.
> Patterns of suburban shadows stretch away
> under the brightness of the Pleiades,
> between the dark continents of cloud that merge
> in the time it takes to smoke a cigarette.
>
> Somewhere a politician looks up "bayonetting"
> to see if it's spelt with one t or two.
> Somewhere a priest is studying results
> of recent municipal elections.
> The baby sleeps through the subsequent storm
> among prints of elephants and penguins
> while lousy bright-eyed dogs over the road
> hunch between chained gates and lightning.
>
> On the morning after the boy's birth
> the church's grubby window illuminated
> two gas cylinders tucked under the altar
> and steps leading down to a dank, rectangular absence.
> When the talk turns to baptism, I see the child
> a thousand feet higher—a river flowing through
> burnished ironstone pebbles and steep forest.
> The River Sangro, twenty five paces wide,
> shallow as water poured over the hands
> where they say wolves still come to drink at night.

In this, the sixth poem, there is too much for me to comment on, but I quote it to show what this poetry is capable of when it takes a larger breath, and not least the metrication which gives each line a sense of containment while maintaining a strong flow through the poem, with ghostly hints at quatrain end-rhyming. It is not three poems tacked together. The imagery develops from one scene to the next throughout; the shift from dogs to wolves is only the most obvious instance. The conflict between dark (encompassing) and light (bright points) is echoed and translated until it becomes a moral issue, finally resolved into earthly extent. This is how I take it, assuming that the new child is the author's son, being coerced into commitment and ritual (throughout the book the modern church is very much part of the ruins). The final apotheosis of this very particularised night-survey of the city, while it raises attention far above the priestly-political squalor, is couched in a Wordsworthian dialect of precise, measured, and alluring detail which prevents it from being some kind of transcendental inflation. The better baptising, of the hands, the decision not to mention the wolves' bright eyes, sublimity turned back to the earth… This accuracy, sharpened by the figures of the poetical voice, is all over the poem, and all over the book.

Three Poems from *Blueroads* [1]

Derek Slade

My aim in this essay is to look at two lyric poems and a poem sequence from *Blueroads*, to try and identify some of the characteristics of Peter Hughes' earlier poetry, and where appropriate to see how these prefigure the matter and manner of his later work. But to begin on a personal note: *Blueroads* was my introduction to Peter Hughes' poetry. What I found in this collection was poetry of such vivacity, such a range of tones and modes and subjects, above all such an enlivened and enlivening engagement with language and life, that it has kept me reading him with huge delight ever since.

Blueroads appeared from Salt Publishing in 2003. This was a time at which Salt was establishing itself as an important publisher of poets associated with "experimental" or "avant-garde" poetry, putting out either often quite substantial retrospective collections by poets whose work had previously appeared from small press publishers or new collections from such poets.[2] If we take 2003 as the mid-point of a five-year span, we see that poets published by Salt during this period include names like Sean Bonney, Andrea Brady, David Chaloner, Andrew Duncan, Allen Fisher, Bill Griffiths, Alan Halsey, Randolph Healy, John James, Peter Larkin, Drew Milne, Geraldine Monk, Ian Patterson, Simon Perril, Frances Presley, Robert Sheppard, John Temple, Nick Totton and John Wilkinson. (Some of these were to be published later by Hughes' own Oystercatcher Press.)

Blueroads falls into the category of retrospective collection. It brings together poems previously published in pamphlets or chapbooks between 1986 and 1999, though it notably excludes anything from Hughes' first pamphlet, *The Interior Designer's Late Morning*, published by John Welch's The Many Press in 1983. All but two of the first eleven poems in *Blueroads* come from *Bar Magenta*, Hughes' second pamphlet publication (again published by The Many Press, together with poems by Simon Marsh, in 1986). The two exceptions are 'Departure' and 'Bedroom'. Hughes assembled the poems in *Blueroads*, and he chose to make 'Departure' the

---

[1] Peter Hughes, *Blueroads: Selected Poems*, Cambridge: Salt Publishing, 2003
[2] Salt's interests at this time were not limited to such poets, and more recently they have shifted to very different types of writer. But I expect I'm not alone in being grateful to Salt for making available not just work by these poets but also related essay collections and the *Companions* series.

opening poem, presumably an important decision.

Going down to the station: Departure

Going the other way, a Russian goods train
hauls a load of snow towards Padua.

Bonfires of vine prunings haunt the plain.

At the end of the platform a shovel
with its handle split is half-buried,
like aspiration,
in a luxurious pile of cold soot.

(*Blueroads*, p.1)

Waiting at a railway station, noticing things. A brief poem, perhaps slight? The railway station might seem to be a ready-made literary property, an apt location for consideration of one's own position and relationships, both with others and the world, easily involving generative oppositions such as stillness/movement, past/future, then/now, arrival/departure. Having suggested that the circumstances of the publication of *Blueroads* provides a context for Hughes' poetry, I now want to invoke a different sort of context, to get closer to what Hughes is going in 'Departure'. We don't hear so much these days of the "English line" of poetry, running from Hardy through Edward Thomas to Philip Larkin.[3] One type of line that does run through these poets is the railway line: they each have station poems, and in each case the poem discloses something central to the poet. Hardy's is a classic statement of his sense of life as a matter of ineffably diminishing returns:

We kissed at the barrier; and passing through
She left me, and moment by moment got
Smaller and smaller, until to my view
      She was but a spot.
….

---

[3] For Hardy and Larkin, see Donald Davie, *Thomas Hardy and British Poetry*, London: Routledge & Kegan Paul, 1973, especially Chapter 3, 'Landscapes of Larkin.' Also see Edna Longley: 'Edward Thomas and the "English" line', (*New Review* 1:11, February 1975), 'Larkin, Edward Thomas and the Tradition', (*Phoenix* 11-12, Autumn and Winter, 1973-4).

> And she who was more than my life to me
> >   Had vanished quite…
>
> >   ('On the Departure Platform')[4]

In 'Dockery and Son', Larkin makes a show of even-handedly exploring the question of why some people have children and others don't ("Why did he think adding meant increase? / To me it was dilution… Where do these / Innate assumptions come from?") before, typically, finding rueful consolation for his own isolation in his usual common denominator, death: "the only end of age." But the heart of the poem finds him on a station platform:

> >   …waking at the fumes
> > And furnace-glares of Sheffield, where I changed,
> > And ate an awful pie, and walked along
> > The platform to its end to see the ranged
> > Joining and parting lines reflect a strong
> >
> > Unhindered moon.
> >   ('Dockery and Son')[5]

"Unhindered moon" is another characteristic Larkin move, an image intended to signify a largeness of vision, implicitly to raise the poem and more importantly the poet above Dockery's apparently more significant achievement of getting a son: yes, I may be alone, and eat awful pies, but see what I have created. *Ars longa* is hovering in the background.

"No one left and no one came / On the bare platform." If Larkin's unhindered moon seems calculated to reflect favourably on the poet, Edward Thomas's 'Adlestrop' reaches out genuinely beyond its author:

> And for that minute a blackbird sang
> Close by, and round him, mistier,
> Farther and farther, all the birds
> Of Oxfordshire and Gloucestershire.
>
> >   ('Adlestrop')[6]

---

[4] Thomas Hardy, *The Complete Poems*, ed. James Gibson, London: Macmillan, 1976, p.221.
[5] Philip Larkin, *The Whitsun Weddings*, London: Faber and Faber, 1964, p.37.
[6] Edward Thomas, *The Collected Poems of Edward Thomas*, ed. R. George Thomas, Oxford: Oxford University Press, 1978, p.71.

But although Thomas' ideas of England, Englishness and patriotism were far from straightforward, the poem's war-time evocation of England as a matter of

> …willows, willow-herb, and grass,
> And meadowsweet, and haycocks dry

wouldn't go unquestioned now.[7]

So, three English lyric poems I've brought together by virtue of a common setting: telling of diminished expectations, poetry as self-defence, and an idealised view of England as haycocks and birdsong. What does Peter Hughes do with this setting? It's tempting to surmise that the title ('Departure') and the opening words ("Going the other way") announce a determination to move away from just such poetry of the "English line." (Indeed, to do so from the standpoint of an Italian station.) To say this is to link Hughes again with the innovative Salt poets listed above. However, writing about what drew him to publish Hughes' early work, John Welch stresses the individuality of the writing, its refusal to be defined by reference to any particular poetic tendency:

> I was drawn to the clarity and control, the "clean lines" of the writing. It wasn't self-consciously "experimental" but not "mainstream" either. There was an exactness of description, an engagement with the physical world, with moments of strangeness, but not a striving for effect, and no yielding to the pressure or temptation to provide a moment of significant closure.[8]

The clarity and control that attracted Welch are evident firstly in the poem's paratactical structure. Three verses, each a sentence, each containing a dominant image: a moving train, smoke drifting across the landscape, a shovel half-buried in a pile of soot. Each verse has a distinct effect.

> Going the other way, a Russian goods train
> hauls a load of snow towards Padua.

Hughes can be a very funny poet, indeed, he's one of the few poets who can make me laugh out loud. Here though the humour is understated,

---

[7] See for instance his contrast of "a settled, mystic patriotism" with one which is "bombastic, hypocritical or senseless" (from the essay 'War Poetry', quoted in Andrew Motion, *The Poetry of Edward Thomas*, London: Routledge & Kegan Paul, 1980, p.97.
[8] Email to DS, 16 March 2012. Quoted by kind permission of John Welch.

based on a registration of what is seen ("a load of snow") rather than what is known or can be guessed at.

Bonfires of vine prunings haunt the plain.

"Haunt" is one of the most literary words in the language, suggestive of troubled or troubling presences. It brings to the poem a charge of feeling that, while it's not exploited by the poet to glorify his feelings or invite sympathy, quietly reverberates into the final verse.

At the end of the platform a shovel
with its handle split is half-buried,
like aspiration,
in a luxurious pile of cold soot.

This works more complexly than the previous, shorter, verses. If there is a "moment of strangeness" (to pick up another of John Welch's terms) in the poem, it's in the third line. "Like aspiration" stands out for a number of reasons. It's by far the shortest line. It contains the only abstract noun in the poem. It's also the first and only simile. But it doesn't do what we might expect a simile to do, in a poem apparently built around observations: give us the satisfaction of being able to say "why, this presents the object in a new and unexpected way: how vivid and accurate it is! How clever of the poet—and of us, for recognising this." In that case, what does it do? The only answer seems to be that here something of the poet's state of mind is being disclosed. Though why, for him, aspiration is "half-buried", remains a question. If there's any sort of story here it too is half buried. We're not encouraged to speculate (though we can note that the suggestions of "haunt" are flickering about). Instead, we're returned to the shovel and what it's half-buried in: "a luxurious pile of cold soot." Here is an unexpected descriptive term. Asked to insert an adjective into the phrase "a ___ pile of cold soot", it's unlikely that we'd come up with "luxurious". To use another of John Welch's phrases, the line illustrates Hughes' engagement with the physical world. It also demonstrates his engagement with the materiality and history of language, firstly through the deployment of "l" sounds in "luxurious pile" (continuing and concluding a series that starts with "platform", "shovel", "handle", "split") before finishing with the hard terminal plosives of "cold soot". There's also a contrast etymologically: "luxurious" (like "aspiration" just above it) coming from Latin, and "cold" and "soot" reaching back via old English to old Norse.

Thus in 'Departure' we find unexpectednesses of wording; expressive variation in line length; readiness to take language from a range of registers and provenances; alertness to the sound qualities of language; non-prioritisation of narrative. To adopt a recent formulation by the poet and critic John Goodby it is a work by a poet "who sees poems as events in language rather than vehicles for sentiment or anecdote."[9] Another way of putting this is to say that unlike in the poems by Hardy, Larkin and Thomas, Hughes is not finding an experience to fit a conviction.

Displacement, disguise, distance: 'Bedroom'

The second poem in *Blueroads* is 'Bedroom', and as we've seen like 'Departure' it wasn't collected in either *The Interior Designer's Late Morning* or *Bar Magenta*. It was published in the small magazine *Active in Airtime*, no. 4, Summer 1995. However, since the contents of *Blueroads* seem to be arranged in chronological order, I'm going to assume that it was written prior to the *Bar Magenta* poems (a selection from which immediately follows 'Bedroom' in *Blueroads*).

Bedroom

a ripple flits over cold urine
in an old pot

the last field maple leaves
leave the tree

your last breath

your father strides the fields
having hoovered the living room

he weeps with frustration
as your dog wiggles upside down
scrubbing the fur on the back of its neck
into a slightly putrefied bird

---

[9] John Goodby, in a notice posted to the UKPoetry list (UKPOETRY@LISTSERVE.MUOHIO.EDU) on 8 May 2012.

then shakes itself up
walking away with its head held high
in the garland of its new odour

(*Blueroads,* p.2)

Someone has died. Someone else, possibly (and that "possibly" turns out to be important) the dead person's father, has taken a dog for a walk, during which the dog rubs itself into the rotting carcass of a bird. 'Bedroom' might seem to challenge the assertion made above, that Hughes writes poems that are events in language rather than anecdotes: there is a story here, or at least related incidents. Similarly the poem appears to end by illustrating a conviction, that in the face of death life goes on, or that the natural world is oblivious of death (cf. Yeats' "Man has created death"): the dog struts off, delighted with its "new odour."[10] I hope to show, though, that to reduce the poem to such truisms is seriously to sell it short. It's a more troubled poem than such an account would suggest, calling into question the status of the poet and the poem.

Like 'Departure', 'Bedroom' begins by setting down concise distinct images, separated on the page. The chamber pot metonymically evokes a particular social historical context, the falling maple leaves tell us it's autumn. Unlike 'Departure', there is no punctuation in the poem. Reviewing Hughes' collection *Nistanimera* (2007), Peter Riley noted that "there is almost no punctuation in the whole book, a rare procedure these days."[11] If I am right in my assumption about the early place of 'Bedroom' in the time-line of Peter Hughes' writing, this is the first instance of his choosing not to use punctuation. In some poets, notably Tom Raworth, the absence of punctuation often produces deliberate syntactical ambiguity, allowing groups of words to relate back to the previous line and/or forwards to the next. In some of Hughes' later work, such as *The Sardine Tree*, *Collected Letters*, and some of the poems in *The Pistol Tree Poems*, an absence of punctuation creates effects similar to those in Raworth, further complicated when the poems are arranged in side-by-side columns, so that phrases can be read both horizontally and vertically (and sometimes diagonally) in relation to other phrases:

---

[10] W.B. Yeats, 'Death' (*Collected Poems*, London: Macmillan, 1967, p.264).
[11] Peter Riley: 'Tenuous Balances', *PN Review* 180, Volume 34, Number 4, March-April 2008. Page number not given, as I consulted the on-line version, available at http://www.pnreview.co.uk/cgi-bin/scribe?item_id=3240.

```
invisible         harmonic rain
   bows arc         beyond
     our ken        a whinny
```

(*The Pistol Tree Poems*, poem 81, p.118)

```
   it starts   to go
     off        as planned
   to begin    to the end
   to open      & read
the seals      images
```

(*Collected Letters*, [unpaginated, poem 21]

In 'Bedroom' the effect is different, though no less significant for our reception of the poem, as can be seen by inserting punctuation:

A ripple flits over cold urine
in an old pot.

The last field maple leaves
leave the tree.

Your last breath.

This produces a solemnity, a portentousness, that is at odds with the poem as published, where unhindered movement between verses gives a sense of openness that suits the pervasive theme of transience (found in the contrast of "old pot" and "new odour", the leaves falling, the last breath, the rotting bird). End-stopping the verses would destroy this effect.

Although it doesn't conform to traditional definitions of the sonnet (e.g. "A lyric poem written in a single stanza, which consists of fourteen iambic pentameter lines linked by an intricate rhyme scheme"),[12] we can notice that 'Bedroom' is a 14-line poem, and I want to follow Peter Hughes' lead when describing the *Metro* poems by saying this gives it a "sonnet shape."[13] Hughes has been attracted by the sonnet shape at various points in his career to date, and it's notable that his poems in this form are often

---

[12] M.H. Abrams, *A Glossary of Literary Terms*, 3rd ed., Holt Rinehart Winston, 1971, p.159.
[13] In the interview with John Welch included in the present volume ('An Interview with Peter Hughes', pp.13-23, hereafter 'Interview'), Hughes says *The Metro Poems* "hovered around a sonnet shape", p.16, but see the footnote following for the number of sonnet-length poems in that collection.

concerned, like 'Bedroom', with transience, change and time passing:[14]

> though it's true that we won't last for ever
> (*Lynn Deeps*, [unpaginated] poem 10)

> I know the light is becoming thinner
> (*The Summer of Agios Dimitrios*, '7.4 Saturday 27th October')

> I replace the bulb but night keeps falling
> (*The Metro Poems*, 'Arco di Travertine')

And in *The Pistol Tree Poems*, where Hughes and his collaborator Simon Marsh write poems that successively diminish in length by one line at a time, when it comes to Hughes' 14-line poem we find "echoes of dead voices coming in waves" (poem 79).

Thinking of 'Bedroom' as a sonnet, we can see that it features two not quite over-lapping structural patterns, one based on events, the other on division into verses. In terms of events, the first eight lines contain the rippling across the pot, the leaves falling, the last breath, and the father striding across the field having hoovered the living room, and then his weeping with frustration. The last six lines focus entirely on the dog's activities. But this octave/sestet pattern is disguised by the way in which the last six lines are gathered into two verses, one of four lines and one of three lines. The dog's actions can be considered as disguise-making, as we'll see later, and I shall be arguing that disguise comes to have an important thematic place in the poem. At this stage I want to suggest tentatively at least that the idea is presented at the level of form.

We can begin to approach notions of disguise and distancing more closely by considering Hughes' use of second-person personal pronouns in the poem.

> your last breath

---

[14] For examples of Hughes' use of the sonnet shape, see *The Metro Poems*, where 16 of the 31 poems have 14 lines; *Lynn Deeps*, a sequence of 10 sonnets; *The Summer of Agios Dimitrios*, where 7 poems have 14 lines; and most intriguingly, since the poems in it take many apparently wayward shapes, *Collected Letters* has 14 sonnet-length poems. Given Hughes's interest in the form, it was an astute choice by the editor of *10th Muse* to ask him to review *The Reality Street Book of Sonnets* (*10th Muse* 16, May 2009, ed. Andrew Jordan, pp.50-51).

Derek Slade 41

> your father strides the fields
>
> ...
>
> as your dog wiggles upside down

There seems to be no difficulty here. The first "your" refers to the person who has died. "Your father" is the father of the dead person (an identification strengthened by the proximity of the lines and their both beginning with "your"). "Your dog" is the dog that belonged to the dead person, so that it is poignant that it's now the father who takes it for walks. This is all perfectly consistent. But the double-line gap between "your last breath" and "your father..." is just enough to make us wonder whether the referent is actually the poet. In poetry (and not just in poetry), depending on the context, "you" and by extension "your" can have various meanings. Usually it refers to someone other than the poet or implied speaker: an addressee or dedicatee. But as John Hall points out in an essay in *The Gig* 15, it can be "that generalized 'you', equivalent to 'one'."[15] This does not seem to be the case here. However, analysing the Frank O'Hara poem 'Having a Coke with You', Tom Jones shows how in the line "you suddenly wonder why in the world anyone ever did them" the referent of "you" is the poet (blended, it's true, with "the specificity of the other person referred to as 'you'").[16] The flicker of doubt as to who is being signified in Peter Hughes' line is possibly supported by the reference to the chamber pot apparently located in the dead person's bedroom, which, maybe illogically, suggests to me that it is an older person's room. Similarly, the father's doing the hoovering may indicate that it is his wife, rather than a daughter or son, who has died; an interpretation that depends on the presence of a division of labour in domestic work possibly traditional at the time at which the poem is set.

Clearly enough, if this reading is given credence, its effect is to create a sense of distance that would be absent if Hughes had written "my father strides the fields." But even if the flicker of doubt as to the referent of "your" is banished in favour of the consistent reading of the pronouns noted above, we are left with the question, where is the poet in this poem? In his

---

[15] John Hall, 'Eluded readings: trying to tell stories about reading some recent poems', *The Gig* 15, September 2003, ed. Nate Dorward, p.46. The essay is on pages 35-54.

[16] Tom Jones, *Poetic Language: Theory and Practice from the Renaissance to the Present*, Edinburgh: Edinburgh University Press, 2012, p.93. Another potential meaning of "you" in poetry is found in A.D. Moody's commentary on the third of Eliot's 'Preludes'. Moody interprets "you" in the lines "You ... watched the night revealing" and "You had such a vision of the street" as referring to a "persona or alter ego". A.D. Moody, *Thomas Stearns Eliot: Poet*, Cambridge: Cambridge University Press, 1979, p.25.

essay on death in the poetry of Roy Fisher, Peter Robinson says "Death is a creator of simultaneous intimacy and distance."[17] 'Bedroom' begins with a moment of implied possible intimacy: the poet must presumably have witnessed the ripple that "flits over cold urine / in an old pot" (though we note that this isn't the same as writing "the old pot", which would tend to confirm the sense of intimacy). Shortly after, there is the possibility that he was present at the moment of "your last breath", though the last breath may be being imagined, giving the piercing suggestion that the dead person died alone. "Your last breath" being the only phrase in the poem not embedded in a sentence, there is no context to help us decide. So, at these moments, there is simultaneous intimacy and distance. In the poem as a whole, it's the absence of first person pronouns in a poem containing four second person pronouns that produces uncertainty about the poet's place. In the essay already quoted from, John Hall remarks that "There can be no second persons without an implied first person."[18] In that case, who is the implied first person in 'Bedroom'? I've floated the idea that it is the father's son, while admitting that this is only a possibility. At one level it is of course the poet, but his relationship to the other figures in the poem remains undefined or ambiguous.

I want to look finally at the types of behaviour presented in the poem, in particular the behaviour of the father and the dog. The father strides the fields; the death has either already occurred or possibly occurs during the walk. Before going out, he has "hoovered the living room", an activity that can be seen in various ways, firstly as a regular domestic task. But ridding the house of dirt and dust—dead matter—in the presence of actual or imminent human death gives the activity an additional weight of significance, brought out in the quiet pun of "living room" and its implicit contrast with the poem's title 'Bedroom', containing the death-bed. Further, the hoovering can be regarded as a form of displacement activity, undertaken to preserve some sense of normality and continuity, but especially to avoid confronting the fact of death. Another instance of displacement comes with the father's "tears of frustration." On the face of it, these are occasioned by the dog rolling in the dead bird's remains. The father has just hoovered, and now the dog is going to bring into the house the smell of putrescence. It's clear, though, that this is only the proximate

---

[17] Peter Robinson, 'Last Things', Chapter 12, *The Thing about Roy Fisher*, Liverpool: Liverpool University Press, 2000, p.283.
[18] John Hall, op.cit., p.42. I have silently corrected a presumed typo at the start of the sentence quoted, where "The" should be "There".

Derek Slade

cause of the tears; they are actually caused by the death within the house.

In the final lines the dog "walk[s] away with its head high / in the garland of its new odour." We've already seen how this can be read as furnishing the poem with a conclusion that is a convention in many poems about death: a movement or gesture towards life continuing. I think that this effect is present, but that it coexists with a complicating factor, seen when we notice exactly what the dog is doing. There seems to be no generally-accepted explanation for why dogs roll in decomposing carcasses or faeces. One theory is that it is a form of disguise, an ancestral trait deriving from wolves, which engage in such behaviour to mask their scent, enabling them to approach prey without detection. So that the dog, as well as being blithely unaware of the death back in the house, is adopting a disguise, concealing its identity.

In this reading of 'Bedroom' I have attempted to show how, emerging from the presentation of scenes and activities related to a death, and apparent at the levels of form, deployment of pronouns and selection of narrative events, there is a set of interrelated themes: distance, displacement and disguise. The interrelationship is seen in the way that the second and third terms are each involved in creating distance. A displacement activity is carried out when doing a harder thing is difficult, intolerable or apparently impossible; it's a means of keeping the bad thing at a distance, in order to function at all. Disguise is putting something in place of one's true identity, thereby inserting distance between oneself and the world. The question remains, how do these implied themes feed into our understanding of what the poem is doing? John Hall again: "Much of reading is holding nerve in interrogative space."[19] I take it that the phrase "interrogative space" as used here refers to the poem as a site of multiple types, levels and sources of questions both formulated and encountered by the reader in the act of reading. I believe that the function of the themes identified above is to pose questions concerning both reading, and, more particularly, writing about death: if you are writing about death, how and where do you position yourself? Is some form of disguise necessary to approach the subject? Perhaps most radically, is writing about death itself a kind of displacement activity?

'Departure' and 'Bedroom' are relatively early poems by Peter Hughes, showing him using the full resources of the lyric poem to articulate and interrogate experience in a highly individual manner. As his writing

---

[19] John Hall, op.cit., p.52.

develops from this point, his approach becomes more "ludic and improvisational" in John Welch's words ("quirkier" is Hughes' own term), and he moves away from single stand-alone poems to poem sequences and sets of poems.[20] In his review of *The Reality Street Book of Sonnets*, Peter Hughes says "It is full of poems you might actually want to read."[21] These two early poems by Hughes are ones that amply repay not just reading, but re-reading.

Trusting the Art: The Seasons

In this final part of the essay, I'm going to look at some aspects of 'The Seasons' (*Blueroads*, pp.11-16), which received its first pamphlet collection in *Bar Magenta* (1986). As noted above, Hughes' work has increasingly appeared as poem sequences or sets. From *Ode on St Cecilia's Day* (1990) onwards, all or almost all of his published poetry has taken this form. 'The Seasons' is the first of Peter Hughes' poem sequences, and it is worth enquiring why he has been drawn to what John Wilkinson has called "this most characteristic of twentieth-century forms."[22] For Jack Spicer the attraction to what he termed the serial poem was prompted by an impatience with the limitations of stand-alone poems and the recognition that "poems should echo and re-echo against each other. They should create resonances. They cannot live alone any more than we can."[23] I'd guess that this potential for creating meaningful reverberations over a distance was equally attractive to Hughes. I'd further hazard that his experiences as a jazz saxophonist and a visual artist also contributed, both practices permitting a blend of free improvisation and recurrent motifs. In an essay on poetry pamphlets, Hughes has commented on the particular satisfactions offered by the poem sequence, especially when published as a pamphlet (as most of his have been):

---

[20] The email from John Welch to DS quoted from earlier (see footnote 7, above) ends with the sentence: "The more ludic and improvisational aspects of his work came along later." Peter Hughes has said of *The Metro Poems* that "[they] were quirkier than my earlier writings". ('Interview', op.cit., p.16.)

[21] Peter Hughes, *10th Muse* 16, May 2009, ed. Andrew Jordan, p.50.

[22] John Wilkinson, *The Lyric Touch: Essays on the Poetry of Excess*, Cambridge: Salt Publishing, 2007, p.110.

[23] Quoted by Ian Brinton, 'Jack Spicer's Words: "God must have a big eye", *Tears in the Fence* 52, Autumn 2010, ed. David Caddy, p.115.

> Many of the best are complete sequences. There is something particularly satisfying about a compact, coherent whole and it is easier to achieve this unity of purpose and organisation in a pamphlet than in a full-length book.[24]

Poem-titles raise expectations, which may be subsequently fulfilled, modified or deliberately dashed as we read through the poem. A first-time reader of 'The Seasons', noting the title, the fact that the first poem is numbered, and also, if her eye slips to the end of poem I, the reference to 'Spring', might justifiably assume that this is going to be a poem in four parts, each part in some way dealing with or taking off from a season in the meteorological sense, probably in the sequence spring/summer/autumn/winter. If this were the case, the title would have given a strong indication of the kind of coherence and "unity of purpose and organisation", referred to by Hughes above, that the poem will display.

But this isn't the case, or not quite (Peter Hughes: "I am not interested in a poem which seems entirely envisaged from the start".)[25] The poem turns out to be in six sections, only three of which make explicit reference to the meteorological seasons ("Spring unbuttoned its wet mac", poem I; "In Summer shirts get dirtier", poem III; "My birthday's in the Autumn", poem IV), leaving three sections where there are not even implicit seasonal markers, suggesting that a search for an organisational principle will have to look elsewhere. Before saying where I think this to be found, I shall quote two passages from the seasonal references just noted.

> You were saying that someone had forgotten
> to wind up the mallards and swans
> when, daft as a grebe's tuft,
> Spring unbuttoned its wet mac.
>   (poem I)

Ducks and swans as clockwork toys. "Daft as a brush" neatly turned. Spring figured as a dirty old man, bringing a new twist to being exposed to the weather. The lightness of touch, the humour, the delight in tweaking familiar phrases and ideas, all coupled with precise observation—this is a characteristic and highly attractive mode in Peter Hughes' writing.

This verse from the autumn passage is no less notable, though the tone is less playful:

---

[24] Peter Hughes, 'Food for Thought', published on The Poetry Book Society website, October 2010. Available at: http://www.poetrybooks.co.uk/poetry_portal/peter_hughes_food_for_thought.
[25] 'Interview', op. cit., p.22.

> Dew and new mushrooms glimmer by garden trees—
> matted, tended surfaces penetrated by cold stalks
> shedding spore white in the postman's footprint.
> You tidied laundry, pens and hair
> turned toast, eggs and pages balancing
> October light on the inside of your wrist.
> (poem IV)

Again, precise observation of a particular point in the year, now calmly done in somewhat longer lines registering the outer world of dew and trees and the inner world of making breakfast while reading (or writing); the two worlds beautifully brought together in "balancing / October light on the inside of your wrist."

As it happens, the two passages just quoted give us a clue as to what is happening in the poem as a whole. "You were saying", "the inside of your wrist." Every section in 'The Seasons' features "you" or "your"; we also find "I", "we", "our". There are episodes of togetherness throughout, whether out in the world—feeding ducks, shopping, kite-flying—or domestic scenes: hanging out washing while the other person laughs from the kitchen, and afternoon love-making. There is intimacy, tenderness, desire, happiness here, recalling Hughes' comment distinguishing himself from some kinds of avant-garde writing: "a lot of innovative poetry is still prim. It is suspicious of humour, sex and the intoxicated. I would like to ship in more of those things."[26] Not that the tone is uniformly celebratory; there are hints that there may be a worm in the bud. In poem III the speaker is drinking wine as he washes his shirt: it's Marzemino, famously the wine Don Giovanni calls for before being taken down into hell, in Mozart's opera. Earlier in the same poem a dog is noticed:

> The white terrier squats on the dusty verge
> uneasily turning her head as the metro
> soars beneath her away from the centre.

A sharp snapshot, but it also more generally suggests that it's not just the dog who vaguely and uneasily senses that something is going on beneath the surface. Lastly, in poem VI the couple are on a ship

---

[26] 'Interview', op. cit., p.22. Also see Barry MacSweeney's letter to the editor of *The English Intelligencer*, where he complains that he is "still looking for more love poems in TEI (& elsewhere)". Quoted in *Certain Prose of the English Intelligencer*, ed. N. Pattison, R. Pattison, L. Roberts. Cambridge: Mountain Press, 2012, p.139.

Derek Slade

>   launching kites, performing
> Punch and Judy for the crew.

They are like puppets because they appear suspended from the kite-strings; but like Punch and Judy they may be having a marital bust-up.

The account above suggests that 'The Seasons' is the story of a relationship, and that I have therefore been guilty of what Veronica Forrest-Thomson terms "bad naturalisation", conveniently summarised by James Keery as "exploit[ing] everything to hand… in order to extract, or construct, a conventional narrative."[27] In fact, Peter Hughes works quite hard to undermine any sense of a conventional narrative. In the first place, there is no apparent chronological sequencing, and thus no beginning-middle-end structure. The most we can say is that the poem presents moments or episodes from a relationship (which returns us to the title and enables us to understand "seasons" as "periods of indefinite or various length").[28] There is also calculated indeterminacy at a number of levels. As in 'Departure', there are times when the referent of personal pronouns is unclear or ambiguous. Hughes uses the potential of the poem sequence to make cinematic cuts and jumps in location, though not only between sections but also within individual poems: poem VI begins aboard a "great ship", clearly at sea, but within four verses and with no narrative link, we have an angler whose "float punctures the river's sheen." Jumps in space are complemented by switches in verb-tense during poems, as in poem V, where there's movement from past ("My warmed up roll had the Union Jack / on a stick stuck on it") to future ("a couple of pounds of petrol will carry you up') to present ("we wobble back from the sunset").

And if bad naturalisation is characterised by a rush to find narrative and to make sense in terms of the empirical world, at the expense of considering "poetic artifice", Hughes ensures we never forget the status of 'The Seasons' as a poem, and not another thing, by weaving into the sequence allusions and references to poems and poetry.[29] Since these constitute some of the most intriguing aspects of the poem, I shall conclude by looking at how they work.

---

[27] James Keery, 'Plight, Magnificence, Stacking and Proximity: The Poetry of Anthony Barnett', in *The Poetry of Anthony Barnett*, ed. Michael Grant, Lewes: Allardyce Book, 1993, p.87.

[28] *Concise Oxford Dictionary of Current English*, ed. H.W. and F.G. Fowler (5th ed.), Oxford: Oxford University Press, 1964.

[29] Veronica Forrest-Thomson, *Poetic Artifice: A Theory of Twentieth-Century Poetry*, Manchester: Manchester University Press, 1978, *passim*.

Poem I begins by setting a scene, blending a familiar descriptive mode and a possibly unfamiliar term:

> Night squats to listen as the boiler
> starts playing chanter to the local dogs.

The personification of night may remind us of how Eliot begins his poem sequence 'Preludes': "The winter evening settles down."[30] "Chanter" here means not one who chants but the melody-pipe of a bagpipe, capturing the wheezing and whistling of the boiler. What follows may bring us up short:

> Metaphors trundle up the garden path
> like bison on roller skates.

This is very funny, a cartoon picture. But does the comic incongruity signify a dissatisfaction with figurative language, so often regarded as a staple, if not the defining feature, of poetic language?[31] And so soon into the poem? In that case, how do we explain the metaphor in the next verse: cigarette butts on the edge of an ashtray are "stocky doubled-up sailors asleep on the moon", which is vivid, witty, humorous but not ridiculous. But the ashtray itself is involved with this putative theme of poetry and incongruity. It is, strangely, inscribed with a translation of a phrase from Rilke: "I believe in nights", and thus seems to be an unsettling comment on the place of poetry, as fit for souvenir items.[32]

Elsewhere, Hughes enlists Keats' 'Ode to a Nightingale' to produce comic bathos in the transition from sensuous description to thinking about getting to work:

> The water edge sounded through soaked gravel
> below each separate leaf, minutes from
> the beginning or end of all vespers.
>
> Vespers! the very word recalls the second hand
> scooter that carries you to your temporary
> bar job.   (poem IV)

---

[30] T.S. Eliot, *Collected Poems 1909-1962*, London: Faber and Faber, 1974, p.23.
[31] Why are the metaphors like bison, when many other nouns would have produced a similar effect of incongruity? No doubt a coincidence, but the reference to chanter as part of a bagpipe may take us to Louis MacNeice's 'Bagpipe Music', where we find "Their halls are lined with tiger rugs and their walls with heads of bison". *Poetry of the Thirties*, ed. Robin Skelton, Harmondsworth: Penguin Books, 1964, p.72.
[32] "Ich glaube an Nächte", from 'Du Dunkelheit, aus der ich stamme', in *Stundenbuch (Book of Hours)*. Accessed at http://www.beyond-the-pale.co.uk/rilke.htm.

Poem V also brings together comic bathos and allusion:

> My warmed up roll had the Union Jack
> on a stick stuck in it. Affecting
> to assemble snugly ham and tomatoes
> it really merely held the cheery
> rectangle and formed an occupied hole.
>
> Then as I considered everything
> that didn't grow and your green
> tights it stabbed me in the gum.

The primary allusion here is to Luke 12:27: "consider the lilies how they grow; they toil not, they spin not, and yet I say unto you, that Solomon in all his glory was not arrayed like one of these." As the speaker is looking at his partner's green tights, this is a nicely turned implicit compliment. The frank appreciative gaze also strikes me as a John James moment; I'm thinking of James' lines such as "her bright green leather high-heeled pumps."[33] The comedy is all to do with the ham roll. It is prefigured in the language ("stick stuck… really merely held the cheery") and climaxes as the speaker's erotic reverie is rudely punctured: "it stabbed me in the gum." But how funny is it for a poet to be wounded in the mouth? And how significant is it that the stick holds his national flag?[34] The passage is a near reworking in comic mode of J.H. Prynne's line "I draw blood whenever I open my stupid mouth", which Simon Perril cites in commenting about Prynne's early work that "utterance is… maimed and wounded by a self-conscious sense of inappropriateness and inadequacy."[35]

The passages discussed above present poetry in contexts of incongruity, possible dissatisfaction, comic bathos and harm. Doubt is expressed about the place of poetry. This theme culminates in an extraordinary passage in the final poem of the sequence. The speaker is shaving himself in a mirror on board the ship where, as we noticed earlier, he and his partner have been "performing / Punch and Judy."

---
[33] John James, 'The Dragon House', *Collected Poems*, Cambridge: Salt Publishing, 2002, p.119.
[34] Peter Hughes: "I don't feel particularly 'British'. Maybe because my mother is Irish. Maybe because I feel more at home in a European context". ('Interview', op. cit., p.22.)
[35] Simon Perril, 'Hanging on Your Every Word: J.H. Prynne's "Bands Around the Throat" and a Dialectics of planned impurity', in *A Manner of Utterance: The Poetry of J.H. Prynne*, ed. Ian Brinton, Exeter: Shearsman Books, 2009, p.83. The link between mouths and poetry is given a characteristically humorous twist by Hughes in poem 33 of *The Pistol Tree Poems*: "never put anything in your poem that you wouldn't put in your mouth" (p.69).

> The reason for being here
> is to preclude the question and poetry
> looking forwards over your own shoulder.
>   (poem VI)

This is knotty, highly compressed writing, that marks a kind of crisis. It begins apparently determined to make a definitive statement of some importance ("The reason for being here"), though it's not clear where "here" is: being on the ship? Being alive? Being at this particular moment in the relationship? Rather than receiving clarification as we turn the corner of the line-ending, things become more uncertain and unstable. "The reason for being here / is to preclude the question." What question? The previous verse provides no clues. Possibly engaging in bad naturalisation again, we might guess that it is a question about the relationship (given the setting, I can't help but think of Tom Raworth's book-title, *The Relation Ship*). If this is the case, why does the question need to be precluded? Presumably, because it is hard to confront; maybe the cruise was undertaken as a means of avoiding it. But the sentence (and the line) continue:

> The reason for being here
> is to preclude the question and poetry

The syntax allows "poetry" to be understood in two ways. "The reason for being here is [A] to preclude the question and [B] poetry." So that poetry, possibly the practice of writing poetry, is equally important as the reason for being here. But also there is the reading "The reason for being here is to preclude [A] the question and [B] poetry", suggesting that poetry is itself to be avoided. The sentence still hasn't finished:

> The reason for being here
> is to preclude the question and poetry
> looking forwards over your own shoulder.

The last line opens up further possibilities. It can mean "while you look forwards over your own shoulder", so the speaker, by looking in a mirror, is simultaneously looking forwards and looking back as he considers the various reasons and questions. It can also mean that he sees the figure of poetry in the mirror, looking forwards over his shoulder—though the expression on poetry's face is left blank. The passage, having raised questions about the place of poetry in life, in a life, keeps all such questions in play.

Derek Slade

If the three lines just considered represent a crisis, as I suggest above, the last two verses of the poem, and the sequence, provide a form of resolution:

A float punctures the river's sheen
the line looped and acock.
A sideways nudge frees the water.
The weighted float sits straight and deep
its luminous tip fitting the slow current.

A paper sounding-board
beats in the rhythm of the air.
You don't know which is your pulse
which the pluck of the kite
as the winds take you by the hand
then take your breath away.

This is very beautiful writing. It evinces a trust in poetry. As in 'Departure' and 'Bedroom' single images are given a verse to themselves, though here Hughes' treatment is more expansive. Although Hughes has poked fun at an over-zealous tallying of alliteration and assonance in reading poetry, we can't fail to note how the lines are unobtrusively bound together sonically.[36] From the first of these verses: "float... frees", "line looped... luminous", "weighted... straight", "sheen... deep." In the second, "paper... pulse... pluck", "board / beats... breath", "which... winds". Despite the rhythmical and metrical variousness of the lines (though two are iambic: "The weighted float sits straight and deep", "then take your breath away") there's a calm steadiness of movement, probably to do with an absence of grammatical units being broken across line-endings.

Poetry is present as implicit subject-matter in both passages, though without any need to surround it with doubts or questions or comedy. Nigel Wheale has recently noted the "shoals of fish" in Hughes' poetry.[37] Often, fish and fishing are associated with poetry and writing poetry. In 'Lakes', the link is a negative one: "they prefer anglers / to composers & poets."[38] 'To Peter Riley on his 60th Birthday', collected in *Blueroads*, begins "Today

---

[36] Peter Hughes, poem 33, *The Pistol Tree Poems*: "the artistic mass of a poem is the number of alliteration features / times the number of assonance features divided by / the average number of syllables per line" (p.68).

[37] Nigel Wheale, 'Collected Letters: Peter Hughes', *Tears in the Fence* 55, Summer 2012, ed. David Caddy, p.135.

[38] Peter Hughes, 'Lakes', in *The Summer of Agios Dimitrios*, Exeter: Shearsman Books, 2009, p.69.

I tried to think about your poem / but it wouldn't stop turning into fish" and constructs an elaborate but tacit analogy between fish and kinds of poet and poetry: "That's why fish usually have to choose: / be saturated within & without / by the domestic, or venture beyond / with the oceanic heavy drinkers" (p.101). If the angler in the first passage quoted above is a surrogate poet, the lines "the line looped and acock. / A sideways nudge frees the water" may at least obliquely refer to the movement from anxiety to freedom and release I have been positing.

In the second passage, "A paper sounding-board / beats in the rhythm of the air." This is an accurate capture of a kite aloft and the drumming sound as the wind takes it; but it is also a poem on the page, dependent on being sounded out, aloud or in the mind, by a reader. There is a similar moment in 'Ode on St Cecilia's Day': "This line is made of air" and perhaps behind them both stands Basil Bunting: "to trace in the air a pattern of sound."[39] In their gesture, the final four lines reach back further in literary history:

> You don't know which is your pulse
> and which the pluck of the kite
> as the winds take you by the hand
> then take your breath away.

This is both unabashedly romantic and Romantic, both in the association of wind and breath with inspiration, the kite as a kind of Aeolian harp, and the interpenetration of outer and inner. It might seem an unexpected, even a risky, way to end. But Peter Hughes has never been afraid to take risks.

"Trusting the art." My title for the last section of this essay comes from a line in 'Paul Klee's Diary': "you cannot start without trusting the art."[40] I have intended it to bear on my analysis of references to poetry in 'The Seasons'. In conclusion I also want to say that reading these early poems of Peter Hughes teaches us to trust his art, and to follow where it leads.

---

[39] Peter Hughes, 'Ode on St Cecilia's Day', collected in *Blueroads*, p.22. Basil Bunting, 'Preface', *Collected Poems*, London: Fulcrum Press, 1968. No page number.
[40] Peter Hughes, 'Paul Klee's Diary', collected in *Blueroads*, p.81. This line was singled out by Barry MacSweeney for his blurb comment on the back cover of *Blueroads*.

The International Language of Fish

David Kennedy

Two wooden fish
In November 2007, I was invited to attend a one-day colloquium 'The Poet and His Translator', organised by the Baltic Sea Centre in Gdansk. I read some of my poems and Jacek Gutorow read his translations of them into Polish. At the end of the evening, an elderly gentleman came up to me, said something effusive in Polish and pressed into my hand a carved, flat, wooden fish. My hosts explained that he came to all the literary events and presented writers with a wooden fish—"but only if he likes what they say". From what I could make out, the fish was carved out of driftwood. It was simple, naive, and child-like in a Paul Klee manner. I liked mine so much, I asked if I could have another one to take home for my wife.

"the slim fish of memory / that slides in and out of my brain" (Anne Sexton)
The fish are light, almost as light as balsa wood, although the wood is much harder. Both fish follow the same pattern: a flat bottom edge and a vaguely undulating top edge which is notched and serrated in two places to represent fins. Both fish have a mouth, carved to look like they're smiling contentedly. Their eyes have been made by pressing into the wood and then colouring with ink. One fish is 120mm long and tapers from 20mm through 10mm then 5mm to end in a 2mm point. This fish is lighter in colour than the other one. The other fish is 110mm long and tapers from 30mm through 20mm then 15mm then 5mm to end in a 2mm point. This fish is darker than the other one.

'Grow Fins' (Captain Beefheart)
I write that paragraph on the second day of working on this essay. I am listening to Captain Beefheart's *The Spotlight Kid* which has a track called 'Grow Fins'. Here it comes now: "I'm gonna grow fins / 'N go back in the water again / If you don't leave me alone / I'm gonna take up with a mermaid / 'N leave you land-lubbin' women alone." I have the CD reissue which pairs *The Spotlight Kid* with *Clear Spot* and has an insert with Beefheart's portraits of Rockette Morton, Winged Eel Fingerling, Ed Marimba and Zoot Horn Rollo. The portraits are not representations of

the individuals but of, say, Ed's marimbaness or Morton's rocketteness just as the little wooden fish are representations of someone's idea of fishness. Beefheart began making art at age three or four, showing a particular fascination with animals—dinosaurs, African mammals, lemurs, and fish. Fish that have never been in the water, like my wooden fish from Gdansk (although their wood has).

Aesthethics
Perhaps there is an international language of fish beyond the one that goes "hey, trawlers, leave them cod alone!" At any rate, receiving little pieces of art in return for some poems that someone had enjoyed speaks to the complex relationship between language and art, a more complex relationship than just pointing language at art and imagining art's a "story". Or imagining that when a poet writes about a painting or a sculpture there's a kind of struggle going on between visual and verbal media. What ekphrasis brings into play are questions of ethics and temporality. You could save the future using ethics derived from my two wooden fish from Gdansk. Aesthethics.

"the meeting point" (Peter Riley)
Peter Hughes is a poet and a painter and his poetry includes a body of broadly ekphrastic writing that responds to painting, jazz, and improvised music. 'Paul Klee's Diary' and 'Keith Tippett Plays Tonight' are typical titles. But I say "broadly ekphrastic" because Hughes' poetry is rarely a representation of a representation. His ekphrastic writing explores the relationship between different arts in terms of form and the process of making. It is also inextricable from the way his poetry, in the words of Peter Riley's blurb for Hughes' Salt "selected" *Blueroads*, "stages the self with wit and precision at the meeting point of contradictory forces from opposed directions, like the past and the present, high art and underfoot mess, institute and instinct." One gets a sense of this in section 7 of *Minor Yours*: "we painted behind the sink / with half a tin of Duracoat / left over at work as Chet Baker / played *Minor Yours* with Art Pepper". (Hughes 2006) One gets a sense of this in section 6 of *Minor Yours*: "the TVs in a shopwindow remind me / of lyrics foreign to this city / sung by friends relatives / or shabby celebrities". (Hughes 2006) Ekphrasis as the meeting point of contradictory forces and the self ditto constantly restage each other.

Two hand puppets
'Minor Yours' (recorded in 1956 and composed by Art Pepper) can be found on the albums *Chet Baker Meets Art Pepper* or *Picture of Health*. The rest of the band is Richie Kamucha (tenor sax), Pete Jolly (piano), Leroy Vinnegar (bass) and Stan Levey (drums). It's on YouTube with a reproduction of the original Pacific Jazz cover showing a topless young woman covering her modesty with two hand puppets, one of which looks worryingly like an early version of a Teletubby. The same session produced tracks that were issued as *Playboys* hence the photograph you can see on YouTube. 'Minor Yours' uses the same chords as 'Love Me or Leave Me' and is a swinging, mid-tempo, West Coast jazz-style tune. I've decorated to that sort of West Coast jazz myself—it gets you and keeps you going.

Idea ⇆ form ⇆ process
Ideas of form and process and the meeting point of contradictory forces are at the heart of two sequences about painters and painting: 'Paul Klee's Diary', written in the mid-1990s, and the more recent *The Sardine Tree* (2008) which responds in great detail to the art and life of Joan Miró.

'Many Species' (James Harvey & Elfreda Harvey)
Poem by James Harvey; pictures of fishes, birds and bees by Elfreda Harvey. Two folded A4 cards, one with poem, one with instructions for operating the fish. In separate envelopes, three threaded coloured card fish containing birds and bees on thread. "First of all, tie the fishes' top threads to a wire coat hanger [...] Then holding the coat hanger, hitting it the birds and bees come down." (Zimzalla object 013, 2011).

Combine
"The Paul Klee sequence was written 15 years ago. I'd been interested in Klee's work for many years: he was the first painter I felt personally absorbed by and in as an adolescent. I'd seen his pictures in galleries across Europe (especially Switzerland), and in New York. I'd also read a good deal of his writings—poetry, letters, notebooks and his theoretical writings on art. I also very much admired his being able to combine painting, writing and music." (Peter Hughes, letter, 15.08.10).

'The culture has failed' (Charles Altieri)
The Klee and Miró sequences are, respectively, 30 and 42 pages long and can be classified, to some extent, as late versions of the modernist long

poem. They are long poems as opposed to just sequences because material and procedures are reworked and refracted throughout. In a discussion of John Ashbery's approach and attitude to the modernist long poem, Charles Altieri argues that Ashbery's starting point is that "the culture has failed primarily because it has produced us as its only heirs". (Altieri 1978: 654) It's like West Coast jazz: designed for open-top driving along the California coast and now it's good for decorating. In itself, Altieri's reading of Ashbery speaks to a pessimistic postmodernism but it converges with two aspects of Hughes' sequences. First, both sequences grapple with how to define achievement in art and with how that achievement is to be measured against the larger failings of twentieth century history. Second, Hughes writes inheritance and succession into his sequences by making them as much autobiographical as they are biographical and ekphrastic. The Klee sequence reads as a blurred narrative in which it is often difficult to tell whether it is the poet or the painter speaking and sequential temporality is largely abandoned. In the Mirò sequence, the autobiographical material (Hughes) co-exists as a right-hand column which harmonises with, offers ironic commentary on, or sometimes dismisses the main text (Miro).

"Allow the audience to play" (Peter Hughes)
"Another interest addressed by *The Sardine Tree* is the provisional nature of any one act of reading. The layout makes a definitive reading explicitly impossible (it always is, of course). Each page works a bit like a painting because there is no one obvious route through the text. The eye has to scan and manoeuvre. I hope this set up a kind of sympathetic resonance of all the possible readings, all of which are authorised, as it were, and none of which is right. The possible alternatives create a jostling democracy of options, and that is one of the meanings of the work. This throws up an interesting issue when it comes to doing a "poetry reading". In the early '90s I went to a reading Stephen Rodefer did (at the Dark Room, in Gwydir Street, Cambridge) where he read from his wonderful 'Four Lectures'. He projected the text on the wall behind him. I borrowed that idea for reading *The Sardine Tree*. This allows the audience to play with alternative readings, or at least get a sense that alternative readings exist." (Peter Hughes, letter, 15.08.10).

Decreation and perilous singing
Altieri again suggests a fruitful approach to Hughes' sequences when he argues that Ashbery's poetic logic and its working out in longer poems rely on "decreation":

> Decreation I take to be a deliberate poetic act intending to disclose possible forms of relatedness, and consequently other possible grounds for identity and value, sharply different from the host forms, the dramatic lyrics, which the decreation parasitically restructures. [...] Decreation alters the economy of consciousness by exploring new modes of exchange among its used and various coins. (Altieri 1978: 661)

Decreation works with and within dominant modes in order to find new ways of making meaning by subverting expected modes of dramatic and lyric consciousness. My wooden fish from Gdansk were certainly a new mode of exchange but what popped into my mind when I read Altieri was (appropriately enough) the ending of Ashbery's 'And *Ut Pictura Poesis* Is Her Name' from *Houseboat Days*, "so that understanding / May begin, / and in doing so be undone".

I looked up Ashbery's swellegant postmodern rag and found it on the Poetry Foundation website and it wasn't quite how I remembered because I'd forgotten how the poem stages its own self-reflexiveness against "other centers of communication" for which "others" may "desert you". And their desire to desert you is equally as powerful as their desire to understand you. Right next to the poem is a link to Peter Gizzi being interviewed by Ben Lerner. The interview is called 'Poetry at the Threshold: Peter Gizzi on lyric selfhood and the perils of singing'. There's no date on the interview but it refers to Gizzi's *Threshold Songs* as if it's recently published so that must make it late 2011 or early 2012. Gizzi says,

> Singing is a perilous business. What does it mean to be next to oneself, seeing and/or singing one's self in time as a rhetorical figure, disembodied and refigured as an embodied line of verse? To be spoken not just in the act of writing, but to be spoken and present and remain intimately embodied in some posthumous time as well—to accept this haunted occupation of poetry?

It's tempting to make too much of Hughes haunting Klee and Miró or of Hughes being haunted by them. But one wonders whether the sequences are a way of avoiding the exposed feeling of being disembodied in order to be embodied lineally. Also, for a while back there, in the postmodern moment, it looked as if narrative was taking over from lyric. But I think that the late twentieth and early twenty-first centuries will come to be seen as the moment when poets recognised that lyric and narrative were co-dependent plausibilities.

Habitable spaces

Hughes' fold-ins of the autobiographical and the ekphrastic can certainly be read as an example of decreation in action and so too can his explorations of new ways of combining factual narration, soliloquy and heightened lyricism. Crucially, by placing himself and his life in such a context, he raises questions about art and poetry as habitable and usable spaces. Works of art can be likened to spaces or worlds we can inhabit but Hughes' sequences also suggest that artists' lives can be habitable spaces for those who come after them. I do not mean by this that artists' lives tell us "how to live" in a weekend lifestyle supplement sense but rather that they can be read for examples of how an individual is enabled or disabled by his or her experiences. An artist's life shows quite literally how experience can be destructive (stopping work) or productive (producing work). In this sense, artists' lives may come to be seen as "other possible grounds for identity".

"The possible" (Peter Hughes)

"I became increasingly aware that a kind of latent fusion hovered in the back of my mind: not Klee's work *per se;* not my local engagements with individual pieces at specific times and places; there was something else. You could call it a kind of buoyancy, or a shifting set of harmonics. It was always there in the background, quietly evolving. It was supportive, and inseparable from who I was. Actually, I think all artists (all people?) have a set of such enabling affiliations. It's not just a question of *influence*. It's a more profound matter which I think is to do with the development of the self, the mind, and what used to be called the soul. It's to do with an expanded awareness of the possible. Klee has always been one of my key presences (for about 40 years now)." (Peter Hughes, letter, 15.08.10)

"Crystalline humps" (Peter Hughes)

Grounds for identity is a framing concern of 'Paul Klee's Diary', a loosely structured, four part sequence which begins "I made you up" and ends by Klee referring to an approving newspaper comment about himself and with the words "must be time to paint this out". (Hughes 2003: 68, 98) Part 1 shows how the sequence works as whole. There is no chronological account of the artist or narratives of Hughes's engagements with Klee's works. We do get material which seems to quote from Klee's writings and other references (e.g., The Beatles, *Blue Peter*) that signal autobiographical material. If we know something about Klee's art, then there are also references to some its more recognisable stylistic features and subjects: fish, angels, "sleepy crystalline humps" and "skinny trees". (Hughes 2003: 70, 73, 74) The poetry also reproduces the dynamic relationship between cold Northern Europe and the heat of Italy and North Africa that can be read across Klee's art. All this material is organised around a shifting set of harmonics. So, for example, "sleepy crystalline humps" echoes and chimes with "sleep caked with red salt", "sleep was guarded by crumbling / columns of grey salt" and "sleep lined with amber crystal". (Hughes 2003: 70, 72, 74) Similarly, "a squall in the head" can be linked with "solstice winds", "warm gusts" and "storms". (Hughes 2003: 72, 74, 75, 76).

"There isn't any symbolism."
(Ernest Hemingway on *The Old Man and The Sea*)
"Anyway, it's hard to write about from the outside, I find. But it's not hard to inhabit a sense of chiming experiences which fuse with some of their points of inspiration, or latent prompts. I can't now remember how I used actual phrases of Klee's. I had no system. The work is not underpinned by any theory. It is not intended to exemplify anything. Poetry (and painting) for me are bigger than intention, or explication, is able to envisage." (Peter Hughes, letter, 15.08.10)

"latent fusion" (Peter Hughes)
The harmonic structures powerfully convey mental activity and the mind and the self evolving. This is reinforced by the poetry's movements between childhood and adulthood. The intermingling of the poet and subject is not intended to make a simplistic equation between Hughes and Klee or to acknowledge an influence. The effect is more a sense of chiming experiences which turn the poet's fascination with the painter into an enabling affiliation. This is what Hughes means by "latent fusion" and Part 1's recurring imagery of sleep, cellars and darkness serves to make such latency clear. We read a record of latent prompts:

> as for us
> sometimes even galaxies which collide
> being mainly space & silence
> simply pass through each other
> with just a few local clicks & flickers
> 	(Hughes 2003: 76)

Dreaming Fish: A Magnetic Game of Water Dreams
(Christine Kennedy)
Handmade edition of 5 magnetic fishing games. Each comprises 10 miniature books with poetry and prose and colour inkjet printed covers and metal studs, colour-printed folding aquarium and magnetic fishing rod. Supplied in silver card box with printed label and instructions. (The Cherry On The Top Press, 2009).

Ekphrasis and outer space
Ekphrasis and outer space is quite the sub-feature of some recent ekphrastic writing. In Simon Denison and Philip Gross' collaboration *I Spy Pinhole Eye* (2009), the systole/diastole movement the pinhole camera's tiny aperture and the allusive nature of the images its produces is paralleled a movement in some poems between micro and macro. Words like "atoms" (49), "grain" (57) and "spores" (74) are contrasted with "the black of space" (29), "impartial stars" (64) and "galaxy" (70). Similarly, Jeremy Hooker's poems in response to Lee Grandjean's sculptures also use a vocabulary of "nebulae", "stars", "collapsing stars", "galaxy" and "planetary". (In Grandjean and Hooker 1998: 24, 28, 30, 31) This makes one wonder whether non-figurative art inspires poets to write about a sense of human locatedness. If figurative art suggests a narrative for the self to be located in then non-figurative art leaves only the vaster, more abstract sphere. This abstract sphere can be related to the fact that both poets are, to some extent, responding to art that converges with Jean-François Lyotard's argument that art that is truly modern is devoted "to the fact the unpresentable exists" and works "To make visible that there is something that which can be conceived and which can neither be seen nor made visible." (Lyotard 1993: 43) Grandjean sculpts wood into objects that do not exist anywhere in the world; and, in a similar sense, Denison's photographs seem to allude to the unpresentable both through the procedure that makes them and the way in which they focus on a small piece (the footing) of a much larger and much more familiar object (electricity pylon).

"interpenetrating universes" (Peter Hughes)
The remainder of 'Paul Klee's Diary' proceeds using the harmonic way outlined above although recognizable Klee material and references to painting increase in quantity and clarity. The quick, fragmentary notations of Part 1 give way to longer paragraphs of verse and clearer portions of narrative. As in Part 1, the harmonic structure offers more than one obvious route through the text. Even so, there seems to be a clear concern with how

description of the world and, by extension, painting can be, in the words of Part 3, "a picture of my mind / a bit of the universe". (Hughes 2003: 84) Elsewhere, it is painting as opposed to physics that is intimate with "the business of parallel & interpenetrating universes". (Hughes 2003: 90) These universes are figured throughout the rest of the sequence as Klee/Hughes, past/present, and life/art. The overall effect is that, as Hughes has remarked in correspondence with me, "Poetry (and painting) for me are bigger than intention, or explication, is able to envisage." In other words, traditional ekphrastic modes are always destined to fall short of their objects or do them a disservice by deducing narratives or morals. The Klee sequence ends with the artist achieving an identity as a painter during World War 1 as "each petty nationalism stands / with a bucket of guts in its hand". (Hughes 2003: 98)

"keep the fish (the foreign language) alive in the water (the culture from which the language was originated)" (Han Liu)
"The Miró sequence has many similarities, although there are significant differences too. After years of admiring Miró's art, I spent some time in Barcelona and thereabouts. I also read what I could of his writings. The letters were especially important, together with a couple of published interviews. My own written exploration of Catalonia merged with notions of beginning and beginnings. I also found myself echoing certain shapes from Miró's art in the disposition of patterns of text on the page. At times, the right-hand column of text also functioned like a musical descant, in harmony with the text on the left. At other times it seemed to offer an ironic commentary, an embittered dismissal. Aspects of this reflected the bloody splits in Spanish history. There was also a desire to explicitly establish some formal distance from an untroubled lyric "I" (which I never use anyway)." (Peter Hughes, letter, 15.08.10)

Fields, fields
The Sardine Tree also places art against conflict with references to the Spanish Civil War and World War Two. There are many similarities with 'Paul Klee's Diary', in particular the interweaving of the poet's and the painter's lives. Two of the poems start with years and Miró's and Hughes' respective ages, e.g. '1983   89   27' (Hughes 2008: 41) There is a contrast between art and physics: "it wasn't until / many decades later / that physicists / were able to find / my paintings in the world". (Hughes 2008: 31) Where the Klee sequence referred to colour's "heady musical tastes" (Hughes 2003: 94) so Hughes has Miró calling his canvases "fields

of sound / fields / of calligraphic & / musical rhythm". (Hughes 2008: 11) Similarly, in Kandinsky's paintings "at last [...] you could listen to music / & read a great poem". (Hughes 2008: 21) Finally, where 'Paul Klee's Diary' had an "internalized" southern Europe (Hughes 2003: 95) so the second page of the Mirò sequence portrays cave paintings as "the animals presented on the rock / stir within us & are found". (Hughes 2008: 2)

"alien air" (Peter Hughes)

But there some striking and significant differences too. *The Sardine Tree* uses Mirò's letters, other writings and published interviews with the artist. So, where the voices of poet and painter were often hard to distinguish in 'Paul Klee's Dairy', here they are much more distinct. The form of each individual poem makes this distinction: a left-hand column presents the reader with a free verse poem in the artist's voice while a right hand column presents the reader with something much more fragmented. The right hand text might give us fragments of the poet's autobiography or refer to art practice in a way that harmonises with the left hand poems and produce, in the words of the sequence, "a tangible descant". (Hughes 2008: 6) Sometimes, as Hughes himself notes, the right hand texts offer ironic commentaries or even dismissals. Crucially, the right hand texts often function as concrete poems that echo shapes from Mirò's art. We get, for example, descending curved lines of varying thickness. The overall effect of this layout is, in Altieri's terms, decreative: any reading must entertain multiple possibilities produced by the text as the meeting of contradictory forces. One can read the left hand and right hand poems separately; as main text and supplement; as main left text and right commentary or vice versa; or one can read across the line so that a single fragmented text is produced. The eye has to scan and manoeuvre rather as it does when one looks at a painting:

> *the song of the vowels*   aeolian aerials
>   orgasm &
>   or a line of your choosing   pain along the edge
>   it took only a moment to make this line   quietly
>   but years of reflection to grow the idea   in a town
>   or caravan
>   I hate the closed line   the belt two sizes too small
>   I hate the frontier   unless I'm leaving
>   but most of all I hate constipated   yob[2]
>   editorials about expanded community   alien air
>   (Hughes 2008: 20)

It is not just a matter of linguistic relationships, e.g. the distant chiming of "aeolian aerials", "editorials", and "alien air". We are invited to read spatially, scanning as we might read a map. The spaces in the text are routes rather than gaps. And the text-as-habitable-space converges with the idea of the artist's work-as-habitable space.

"walk between the title and the picture" (Peter Hughes)
Looking at art is, then, a matter of making readings, a question of taking a "walk between the title / & the picture's substance". (Hughes 2008: 14) This process keeps on happening, hence the sequence's concern with beginnings. We get not only impressionistic narratives of the artist's early life and how he began painting but also of what prompted certain key stages in his art: "in 1973 / I discovered you can burn the canvas"; "when I was asked / to make these two UNESCO walls / I saw baked earth in caves in Altamira"; and "I first did ceramics in 1945". (Hughes 2008: 19, 32, 34)

Why I Am Not
As with Frank O'Hara's poem 'Why I Am Not A Painter', the works produced by making art, writing, and writing about art are parts of larger processes. This means that Hughes' sequence has another curious effect. The ekphrastic poem usually assumes a relatively stable, authoritative speaking "I". As a consequence, we expect that, in the words of Michael Benton, "the poem [will] deflect or deepen attention in respect of its visual catalyst." (Benton 1997: 367) But something else happens in *The Sardine Tree*. The left-hand texts are, in terms of form, relatively stable but the right-hand texts are much less so. As the example quoted above demonstrates, the right-hand texts often deal with displacement and disorientation. This means that the sequence acts as a textual and visual catalyst for its own formal distance from a standard ekphrastic or lyric "I".

Visual unwriting
The visual aspect of the sequence means that it can be read in terms of Hans Lund's category of "integration" where pictorial elements are part of the visual shape of a literary work. The pattern poem or concrete poem aspects of Hughes' sequence clearly echo some of the distinctive shapes we find in Miró's art so that we are given an experience where looking and reading are blurred. The unstable texts that result do not mean that painting has triumphed in the alleged struggle between visual and verbal representation. Rather, in the words of the Klee sequence, these different orders of representation are found to be "interpenetrating universes".

Writing in response to art, to the lives of artists, and to artists' working processes has become a way of rewriting or even unwriting the expected poetic self.

The Golden Fish (Paul Klee)
1925. Oil and watercolour on paper, mounted on cardboard, 50 x 69cm (19⅛ x 27 in). (Kunsthalle, Hamburg)

Reframe constant repair
In many ways, Hughes's poems are typical of a wider turn in which contemporary poets reframe the continuing history of ekphrasis so that ekphrasis becomes a form of critical knowledge that, in turn, reframes the history of criticism. In the face of art's never-ending circulations, writing offers a moment of relief, a rest that can almost literally be grasped and used as a communicating object, an object that then circulates its own new restlessness. Ekphrasis and its subjects are signs under constant repair.

"…fish of memory…" (Anne Sexton)
And have I said how I keep thinking there's a "language of dreams" sort of connection between the notches on my two wooden fish from Gdansk and the parallel lines that Peter Hughes drags across his paintings?

"with your face" (Peter Hughes)
"I've gone on to explore further the shaping of poems on the page. *The Pistol Tree Poems*, *Behoven*, and a recent sequence called 'Site Guides' (inspired in equal measure by Heine and the Caravan Club) all develop this idea. You might be interested to have a look at the opening pages of my Shearsman book *Nistanimera*—it's a group of 6 Klee paintings, a poem for each. I'll leave you with the final three lines of my Salt book, *Blueroads*:

> *I can't help thinking*
> *you can't help looking*
> *at paintings with your face"*

(Peter Hughes, letter 15.08.10)

Bibliography

Altieri, Charles, 'John Ashbery and the Modernist Long Poem', *Genre*, Vol.XI, No.4 (1978): 653-87.

Ashbery, John, *Selected Poems* (London: Paladin, 1987).

Benton, Michael, 'Anyone for Ekphrasis?', *British Journal of Aesthetics*, Vol. 37, No.4 (October 1997): 367-376.

Grandjean, Lee and Jeremy Hooker, *Groundwork: Sculpture by Lee Grandjean and Poems by Jeremy Hooker* (Nottingham: Djanogly Art Gallery, 1998).

Gross, Philip, and Simon Denison, *I Spy Pinhole Eye* (Blaenau Ffestiniog: Cinnamon Press, 2009).

Hughes, Peter, *The Sardine Tree* (Old Hunstanton: Oystercatcher Press, 2008).

Hughes, Peter, *Nistanimera* (Exeter: Shearsman 2007).

Hughes, Peter, *Blueroads: Selected Poems* (Cambridge: Salt Publishing, 2003).

Liu, Han, 'Keep the Fish Alive in the Water: Foreign Language Education and Cultural Understanding in Global Contexts', *International Journal of Humanities and Social Science*, Vol.1, No.11 (August 2011): 207-9.

Lyotard, Jean-François, 'Answering the Question: What is Postmodernism?', in Thomas Docherty, ed, *Postmodernism: A Reader* (Hemel Hempstead: Harvester Wheatsheaf, 1993): 38-46.

ET: the missing letters of Peter Hughes' *Behoven*

John Hall

I am to write a few thousand words on Peter Hughes' *Behoven*, a poem-sequence in 32 parts that fits easily on 32 pages, one for each, making use of far fewer words than this essay. After the pleasures of my first readings of the sequence I would have been happy with three: Just read it. What could I possibly add? But then, why should you, when there is already too much to read? So let me try something a little longer. Read it, in the expectation of any number of lyrical pleasures, for the ear, for the play of line against continuous movement, for its celebration of remembered pleasures, for its good will and for its wit. By this last, I mean a mind in evidence in the poems that can constantly surprise itself in the turns of speech, that can dance in the syllables and still have world and experience in its sights. This could apply to so much of Hughes' work.

The avoidance of an extended response might, of course, be just that: avoidance. I might keep cycling through circuits of pleasure because that saves me from negotiating their salience, their engagement with the space and lives that surround them. In any case, I am going to extend well beyond those two micro-versions of my essay. I shall attempt to write my various readings of *Behoven*, including modes of reading especially designed or adapted for this occasion, and not to pretend that this is an innocent pursuit, since I am myself already written all over, not least by my earlier reading.

§

The title: *Behoven*. Under obligation. Beholden (OED). That's strange. I don't think of Peter Hughes's work as operating under the constraints of debt—of *behoof*. To be behoven is to act in a way that at least acknowledges, possibly even elaborately performs, indebtedness. Poetry can be a proper mode for such a performance. There are instances. But if these particular poems are in debt, who are the creditors? Where gifts, including poetry and music, are exchanged between those who love each other, or are friends, or companions across time and language, creditor and debtor can, like "I" and "you", keep switching roles in alternating polarities of exchange.

I am behoven to every poem and song I love. Of course, the indebtedness is never at any one moment equally balanced.

§

Behoven came out as an Oystercatcher, the series of pamphlets that Peter Hughes himself has been producing since 2008, as folded A4 centre-stapled chapbooks with a colour image on the front of each, usually unattributed, though usually of or from one of his own paintings. In this case, the image is 8 x 10.4 centimetres and may well have been produced on a computer, though photographic transfer makes it difficult to know for sure. The ground is unvariegated black. Superimposed on this are coloured arcs and swirls and one dotted wiggle. The most prominent arc is in differing shades of ochreish brown, arcing almost from bottom left to top right, over a quarter of the width of the whole image, and itself containing further shapes, marked through distinctions of shading and implied layering. The other, slighter marks and gestures are in blues or white. Light seems to come through the brown and through the thin and dotted whites and the lighter blue, suggesting screen rather than reflections off paint on canvas. The darker blues are streaks in the darkness. The whole is full of movement, gesture, traces of, or notations for, imagined past and future actions.

On the recto that faces publication details, there are three lines of italicised text, set a little below the top margin. The page is otherwise blank, as is its verso. This is a vestibule, a space to pass through, to adjust and prepare for the poems ahead. Here are the lines:

> *These registrations of the 32 Beethoven*
> *piano sonatas were made at Oystercatcher*
> *Studios in September and October 2009.*

So it could well be to the 32 piano sonatas of Beethoven that these poems are be()hoven. There is an implied correspondence between 32 numbered sonatas and 32 numbered poems. But what kind of correspondence? "Registration" must be part of the answer, and two of its many senses might help. One is the way it is used in phrases like "her face registered surprise", where the registers are the expressive marks or signs—very likely spontaneous—of emotive response. Guided by this sense, Hughes' registrations would be his—perhaps spontaneous—responses to the sonatas: poetic equivalents of facial expression. I'm more or less happy with that, though I do have two reservations. Firstly, all of Hughes' poems are short and look unified on the page, whereas Beethoven's sonatas use a structure that sets at least two movements, more usually three or four, against each other, and they are much longer than Hughes' short poems. Spontaneous registration might be expected to trace through time the changes between movements and the contours within them. Secondly, "made" and "studios" together suggest an art process. And here another sense of "registration" comes to mind: as a term used in screen-printing for that part of the process that is aimed at ensuring the alignment of image and frame, especially when different colours require more than one pass. If and how this analogy actually might apply, may or may not become clear. In the reading of poems, such a speculation is not a hypothesis to "test" so much as part of an array of expectations of potential, one element in a multiple reading that goes out to meet the poems.

So I am looking out now for two possibilities that do not exclude each other. According to the first, the poet has been listening to all the sonatas in his studio, possibly while painting, and has produced a poem in response to each sonata. The other possibility is that there are more explicit correspondences and alignments, perhaps formal, between numbered poem and numbered sonata. I have already suggested two ways in which correspondence will be lacking: duration and structural complexity. In either case, though, we have some form of ekphrasis, though that term is more usually applied to the transcription of visual material into verbal texts. Given echoes of W.C. Williams in the poems, that poet's *Pictures from Brueghel* (Williams 1963) comes to mind. In that sequence, the correspondence between poem and specific painting is very clear. In *Behoven*, the source is musical and therefore time-based and without any of the explicit referentiality and narrative suggestiveness of the paintings.

§

The shortest *sounded thing* (sonata) in *Behoven* is No.16. Here it is in full:

> he would stalk
>   the winter quarters
>   of the circus
>   glaring at bears

This four-line poem in just 16 syllables, each of whose lines starts at a different horizontal position on the page, forms a syntactically and semantically complete sentence. Supposedly, it is a registration of a sonata in three movements, with the different time signatures and modalities of *allegro vivace, adagio grazioso* and *rondo: allegretto, adagio, presto*. Schnabel's[1] performance of this sonata lasts about 24 minutes. *Allegro vivace* is hardly a stalking measure, nor the *allegretto* or *adagio* of the *rondo* appropriate for glaring, though there may be something graciously at ease—*adagio grazioso*—about the whole.

§

When *Behoven* first arrived, I read through from beginning to end, without resort to recordings of Beethoven or search facilities. Even though I had heard many of the sonatas over the years, I had no conscious memory of their sounded shapes—those scraps of detail held together in a vague gestalt, that seem to constitute musical memory for those of us without a technical map on which to register for later recall our musical experiences. I found that I could download for £1.09 an almost complete set (all except No. 31) of Artur Schnabel's recordings (2009). The sonatas were composed or published between 1795 and 1822, or to put it another way, between the ages of 24 and 51, at an average rate of slightly over one per year. The recordings were made between 1932 and 1935, using a technology manifestly vulnerable to deterioration of quality over time and use, at an average rate of about ten a year. The poetic "registrations" were written over two months in 2009, at an average rate of one every two days.

I don't know which recordings Peter Hughes may have been listening to in his "studios". If this was what he was doing, then his are registrations of the registrations of particular pianist(s), with an alignment of sorts between three different forms of engagement (musical composition, interpretive performance, poetic composition), three historical periods, and over three very different tempos of production. Because languages have built into them many grammatical and lexical devices for invoking relations to time, other modulations of times can come in as tense, mode, aspect, allusion and (lexical) reference within the poems. In *Behoven* 16, the period is unclear: "he" is unlocated and "would" is ambiguous (was in the habit of stalking? was determined to stalk? stalked conditionally?), though bears in the winter quarters of a circus suggest a different time, if not place, just possibly, for all I know, a biographical incident in Beethoven's life.

§

---

[1] See below.

The longest registration is No. 31, at 26 lines. All 32 have a jagged or waving left edge to the text, suggesting a double notational decision in relation to lineation: how to read the fore-space, how to negotiate the break. The syntax usually encourages a projective reading, a movement towards the next line, though I do not mean the term "projective" to suggest affinities with Olson's project in poetics. (1967: 51-61) Lines vary in length but are never long. The visual movement suggested by layout on the page is similar to the effect of that cover image. Lines matter. The notational option of additional line-spacing is used in just under half the registrations, and never in any regular pattern. The impression is of poems mostly as a single movement, without stanzas, but with lines and line-gaps as significant elements in that movement. Higher level devices of repetition, of the kind that suggest themselves to eye before ear, are eschewed, though at the level of phoneme and syllable these become apparent to the ear. The only punctuation is that provided by typographical layout, including horizontal and vertical spacings in relation to implied margins. Higher case is used only for the (relatively few) proper nouns. Two of the poems (18 and 25) include italicised text. With the exception of the repeated "*trampoline*" in 25, these are terms that can be used as musical categories or markings: *divertimento* in 18, *alla tedesca* in 25.

§

Beethoven's name does not appear in *Behoven*, apart from in that prefatory note, though the names of two other musicians do. A catalogue of proper nouns can provide one way of reading almost any text. Here is the complete list from *Behoven*, with the poem's identifying number in brackets: September (2); Bo Diddley, Renoir (3); Maria, Harold (4); Copenhagen, Baltic (9); June, English (10); Vienna (12); Bonn (15); Allegra (18); September, Seine (19); England (24); French (25); Bach (27); Europe (28). Two months; two musicians; one painter; two western forenames for females; one western forename for a male; three European cities; two regions or continents; three countries (as noun or adjective); one river (also a metonym for the city, Paris). Two of the three cities have strong connections with Beethoven: he was born and lived in Bonn until he was 22 and then moved to Vienna (and nearby) for the rest of his life. All the published sonatas were written after his move to Vienna. The poems do not make these connections explicit. Sonatas 24 and 25 were both written in 1809, a year of threat to Vienna—and to Beethoven's hearing—from the continuing military expansionism of Napoleon Bonaparte. "England"

(24) and "French" (25) both, in their very indirect ways, register this context with a reference to negotiations on alliance with England and to nationalism and the French invasion. No. 25 also cites the marking of the first movement of the corresponding sonata: *alla tedesca*, "Germanish".

The three forenames were not of people already known to me outside this poem. Maria and Harold appear in the same line, which suggests that Hughes might have been watching, during a storm that interfered with the television signal, *Harold & Kumar Go To White Castle,* a film from which I have now seen a brief video clip on YouTube.[2] I read the salutation "hail Maria" (4) as deliberately not "Ave Maria" or "Hail Mary" or "Holy Mary" but, in a poem featuring very bad weather, as flirting with the pun on "hail" and as breezily greeting the re-apparition out of the airwaves of a figure from popular culture. This again is not an "interpretation"; it is a possibility that my reading entertains. As for Allegra, Sonata 18 starts, as many of them do, with an *Allegro*. She, Allegra, is introduced by way of a pun on "saw":

> saw a house martin click by
> saw an inch from the black leg
> of the piano for the entry
> of the milliner's cousin Allegra

These lines move towards another pun, on a musical term, that might lead those of us with little biographical knowledge of Beethoven to wonder about the "milliner's cousin":

> feather bobbing to the loo
> in black   deft as in canary
> *divertimento*   road works

And what of Bo Diddley?

> tip-toe between Bo
> Diddley & a Renoir lavender

These are objects, perhaps a vinyl LP and a reproduction of a painting, and they might be nothing but the familiar circumstantial clutter of the "do[ing of] daily matter numerously" (22), like running for the bus a few lines later. More than that, though, Diddley and Beethoven are evidently both parts of Hughes' writing life and there is an indirect connection

---

[2] http://www.youtube.com/watch?v=1Pai7ddaR1w (accessed 16.9.12)

between them through Chuck Berry's *Roll over Beethoven*, where Diddley is referenced, as "diddle, diddle":

> Hey diddle diddle, I am playin' my fiddle,
> Ain't got nothin' to lose.
> Roll Over Beethoven and tell Tchaikovsky the news.[3]

§

So what of the concrete nouns? Hughes' poems are usually full of specifics, of material particularities that are events, repeated actions, recipes or dishes, listenings, sightings (and citings). The world in his poems is both phenomenal and allusive ("literary") rather than speculative and propositional. Concrete nouns snag a world outside language, call on shared cognitive and perceptual knowledge:

> the fact that the song's
> without words
> allows one to continue (18)

Historically, sonatas signified sounded things *without words*. In contrast, Hughes uses words as his primary means: sonatas that go beyond *cantabile* into text. The poems are neither wordless music nor song; they are poems in negotiation with music and song.[4] In place of the keyboard of the piano-forte, Hughes has the keyboard of a computer (at least at some stage in the process).[5] What is it about the piano-forte, that it may become a solo instrument with such potential for thoughtfulness, even though the physical action of striking keys is at an engineered, relayed distance from the hammers that strike against taut wires. Comparable distancing is familiar to writers, no matter what the writing technology they use. A pianist can modulate amplitude, producing soft and low sounds (*piano*) as well as strong ones (*forte*); and can simulate some of the characteristics of blown instruments through varying the force of keystroke and by use of pedals to modulate timbre, colour, volume and duration of notes. The piano is not, however, a "voice instrument", in the way that in some forms

[3] http://www.lyricsfreak.com/c/chuck+berry/roll+over+beethoven_20030907.html (accessed 16.9.12)
[4] I have touched on this question of the relations between poems and songs in "'My head was away and singing': Kelvin Corcoran on and in song' in *The Writing Occurs as Song*, ed. Andy Brown (Bristol: Shearsman, 2013).
[5] In the Oystercatcher pamphlet, No. 32 is reproduced in a facsimile of its hand-written form.

of jazz the wind instruments—especially, the reed ones—can be treated as almost singing words.

§

But what world or what aspects of his world do Hughes' nouns appoint for attention? I shall not attempt a complete list since the category of concrete noun is not nearly so secure as that of proper name and because the list would extend to over 300. I have improvised some categories, for which I have only the clumsiest terms, and shall draw on a quick and impressionistic count from these. For what turned out to be the most populated category, I scribbled down the term *topos*, meaning places, settings, weather and sky, constructions and buildings nameable from without. From No.1, for example, there are *river, jetty, moorings, current*. All of these relate to water, a common element in the sequence in which sky, moon and stars are also often present. River and current, like wind and rain, are natural; jetty and moorings, like *dock* (13), *dockside* (9) and *pier* (24), relate to water-based technologies and economies. Relatively few of the words in this category are specifically urban. Towards the end of the sequence there are *estate* (25), *alleys, streets* (26) and *carpark* (28).

The second most populated category is one that overlaps with the first and to which I tentatively attached the label, "buildings, equipment", meaning buildings, such as a house, experienced from within, together with the *things* of domestic or working life. As examples, No. 7 has *wheelbarrows, sledge-hammers, shorts, piano, bangle*.

The next category is of those nouns that relate to the parts and actions of bodies (including the word *body*). In No 21, for example, there are: *hands, sinuses, lungs*.

Next in frequency are words relating to writing, song and music (for example, *ink, note, song* in No. 6); then to animals (for example, *house martin* and *canary* in No. 18). There are more birds than insects or mammals and two of the animals are exotic rather than domestic—*wolf-cubs* (4) and *bears* (16). My final broad category will be familiar to Hughes' readers: gardening, food and drink (for example, *apricots* and *coffee* in No. 12). Red wine features three times (8, 14 and 29).

One other category, that of nouns that refer to times of day and year, such as *night* (15, 21, 26 (twice), 29, 30) or *June* (10) or, deictically, *tomorrow*, may not technically be "concrete". *Night* is probably the most repeated noun in the sequence (seven times). *Tomorrow* appears three times (though in one instance as an adverb):

> > tomorrow fell from the sky (8)
> > some dust
> > probably settles
> > on the surface
> > of the river
> > tomorrow (23)
>
> > a bell tolls at low tide
> >   with unexpected modulations
> >   of tomorrow (31)

"Tomorrow" is a relationship to and in time from an implied today; it carries an immediate, grounded, sense of futurity. And yet, in the first example it is the subject of a verb in the past tense ("fell"); in the second, it is a paradoxical adverb for present tense ("settles"); and in the third, the only one where tense and "tomorrow" make conventional sense of each other, "modulations of tomorrow" (and of the bell) are "unexpected" from the point of view of a present ("tolls"). Poetry and music both unfold through time, modulating and shaping micro-experiences of time as sounded, according to their differing means. In both, devices of repetition keep past in play and project forwards into the immediacy of expectation.

§

The first movement of Sonata No. 23 ('Appassionata') is playing as I write. I am overcome with unexpected recognition. The movement sets up expectations of modulated repetition that seem to emerge out of the renewed experience; any now carries its own past and future: tomorrow *happened already, is happening in expectation, and is about to happen. The music's enfoldings of time now also enfold my time; this is recognition. And now, thanks to the way digital audio technology transforms the phenomenological time and setting of music, abstracting it from the assemblies and encounters of live bodies for which it was first designed, I have replayed the movement. Writing—and especially printed writing—has long allowed an equivalent: I can easily re-read a poem or part of a poem as soon as I have finished it.*

§

Hughes' No. 1 becomes more particular—more concrete—as it proceeds. The first line is *in medias res* (the time it refers to is already underway when its time of being begins):

> we suddenly lost interest
> in such impossible pasts
> lifting our heads towards
> the river elsewhere

So the poem assumes and refers to a time that it does not include in its own proceedings. I am entrapped in a time that rebuffs me. "We" is often ambiguous, especially, as here, when no candidates for the roles have been placed in either text or scene.[6] These four opening words—these eight syllables—are in a line of their own, suggesting at least as a possibility that this is a self-sufficient statement. Just as "we" can imply a speaker's belonging in any plurality from couple to species and beyond, so the suddenness of "suddenly" is unclear because of the vague, unspecified nature of "impossible pasts". What happens between "interest" and "in", over the first line break? In my case, there is a pause before continuing on with the syntax in a spirit of anticipatory relief that concrete detail will be at last provided, but then "such" again implies that the particulars have already been specified somewhere else and I've missed them. You could say that this poem has already rendered an implied past "impossible" for a reader. How can a past be impossible? Perhaps in the sense that it is a false memory: it couldn't have *really* happened. Perhaps it was a past that did happen but that would have been, it seems now, "impossible", as suggested by the saying, "I couldn't have lived in that time". While attending to those impossible pasts, it would seem from the third line that heads had been kept lowered; that line is nothing like as self-sufficient as the previous two, ending as it does on a preposition ("towards") that is still anticipating its noun. So the syntactical pause follows "heads" but the line continues through an enjambment into "the river elsewhere". If the river is elsewhere, then in this case it has to be imagined or remembered, rather than seen. Then the poem offers a particular image from the past ("stood"), in a line in clear iambic trimeter, as though metric time is mending an idea:

> a new jetty stood beside
> the old beyond repair

---

[6] I shall return later to the pronouns in *Behoven*.

"Idea", quite unspecified, is figured as a boat slipping its moorings (drunkenly?):

> time mends an idea
>   slips its moorings
> swings out into the current

In the poem so far, two verbs have been placed at the beginnings of lines—"lifting" and "swing"—and a few lines later there will be another, "pausing". To my ear, they seem to mimic prosodically what they refer to. After the next few lines I shall have quoted the whole poem, though in pieces:

> & a kneeling figure
> works on
>   pausing only to reach
>   for three more nails
>   & place them gently
>   between her lips

The lineation is a means of line-by-line renewal of surprise through an evident disposition to find both language and world surprising. The poem swings out into a current that moves it. The earlier "lifted heads" are counter-balanced by the "kneeling figure", who turns out not to be in prayer or obeisance but to be getting on carefully—both rhythm and the word "gently" convey this—with a practical task. Only in the last line is the figure gendered. These last lines have some of the joyful mimetic qualities of the well known 'Poem' by W.C. Williams, that starts "As the cat / climbed". (1951: 340). Williams' whole poem is given over to the cat's careful stepping. Hughes, though on nearly as small a scale, works with a more changing, complex structure. This final movement of the poem produces a register shift, offering a coming to rest in the exactitude of three nails placed gently "between her lips". Syntactically and rhythmically, this poem is entirely resolved, though the form and place of resolution may be gently unexpected. There is, in miniature, not only movement but also an impression of micro-movements. Through the way the lines work, they are at one and the same time in sequence and in juxtaposition. The unsettledness of line leaves the time signature uncertain until it is too late and the next has been encountered.

§

While drafting those paragraphs on Behoven 1, *the second movement of Beethoven's 5 was ending. This is marked* adagio molto—*very slow. The ending is gentle but emphatic—that is, signalled as imminent through delays introduced for that purpose. As the end of a second movement, this is provisional. The finale is* prestissimo. *There is nothing gentle about* prestissimo, *though you can swing into its currents.*

§

Concentrating on concrete nouns, as I did above, could suggest an aesthetic like that of the still-life: objects caught in a paradox between sacred and profane through nothing other than a poetic attention that isolates them through naming: poems of *things*. But there are verbs contributing to the movement of these lines: the nouns are active and call for their verbs. Twigs, for example, flick and whip. And what of the verbs? Poetic composition by line can side-step the exigencies of sentence structure, and thereby avoid grammatical reliance on verbs. There are a few examples of this is *Behoven*. A single floating line in No. 29 reads (considerably offset to the right), "correction fluid". This is not syntactically connected to what precedes or follows. And a few lines further down in the same poem, there are a series of compacted phrases that don't quite separate out into clauses or sentences:

> huge wood and ivory wreckage in gulfs
> of red wine its tidal races break another
> bottle on the bows of the self…

This is towards the end of the sequence where such constructions are more frequent. Earlier, in 11, there has been this:

> lethargic topiary
> up beyond the mitten
>   the face in space
> all chapped lips
>   autumn stars

Mostly, though, especially in the earlier poems, the energy of active verbs is consistently sustained. To test this out, I undertook another very rapid and broadly conceived taxonomy and count. I ended up with five categories, on semantic rather than grammatical premises, even clumsier than for the concrete nouns. The first, though not the most numerous, contains the kinds of verbs perhaps expected in lyric poetry, expressing primarily emotive events or states (*lost (1), relieves (3), remembering (9)*), including negotiations with others (*leads* (4), *allows* (18), *negotiate* (24)). I counted 16. The second are verbs that are perhaps the complements to the concrete nouns: verbs of specific physical actions, such as *flick, whip (2), creep (11)*. I found 93 of these, half of them in the first 11 poems. The third are more generalised conceptions of action, such as *mends, works* (1), *brought* (3). I found 59 of these. Fourth, omitting the verb "to be", are verbs of more or less steady state such as *breathe* (12, 26), *live (6), stands (32). I found 23* of these. Finally, the fifth category are verbs of perception, cognition, utterance and communication, such as *peeps* (23), *saw* (18, 24), *thinks* (20, 27), *sing* (3, 9, 28, 30). By my count there were 29 of these.

I wouldn't want these numbers to carry any sense of conviction. Anyone else would group them differently, even using the same headings. But this crude taxonomy confirms that the emphasis in *Behoven* is on action rather than state. Not surprisingly, the verbs are mostly in active voice. A very quick scan of the identified verbs in the first 11 poems suggests that over two-thirds of them have taken a northern or Germanic route into the present-day language rather than the Romance or unknown route of the rest. Given the economic and political histories that have shaped English, this is not surprising and may just be another way of saying that these are poems that deal with physical movement in the world rather than with administrative, political, judicial, scientific or philosophical matters. The stressed monosyllables of many of these verbs makes the kind of contribution that Hopkins might recognise, though quite deliberately, I would say, without his intensity.

§

The last brief survey I wish to make is of the use of personal pronouns in the sequence, ignoring "it" and "its". If the sequence has a pronominal key, it is the un-numbered second person rather than the first person singular. In the 32 lyric poems there are only 9 instances of "I" and none of "me" or "my". There are only two instances in the first 23 poem, one of which is in reported speech, as is the "we" that follows:

>   it wasn't what
>   I thought
>   he said
>   we do (20)

Bearing in mind that "you" can operate as an indefinite pronoun substitutable with "one' and can even offer a way of avoiding saying "I", there are 17 instances altogether (*you*, 8; *your*, 8; *thy*, 1). The first person plural occurs 9 times in all (*we*, 8; *us*, 0; *our*, *1*). There are two male third person singulars and 5 female. *They* occurs 3 times (no *their*).

The third poem offers an early clue about this paucity of pronouns in a world of particulars. This is how it opens:

> screw up page & wipe stars
> appear & tighten
> screw on loft ladder
> tip-toe between Bo
>   Diddley & …

Hughes enjoys putting words into positions of grammatical uncertainty. Here four factors contribute: line breaks, omission of punctuation marks, elision of pronouns (or possibly of the prepositional "to" of an infinitive), and punning. Unless a pronoun is assumed to be elided, "screw up" sounds like an imperative. If a missing pronoun is implied, the verb is active and in the present indicative, and the missing pronoun cannot be "she" or "he" (the verb form would have to be "screws"). The same uncertainty applies to "wipe". That line is rhythmically self-sufficient so it is obvious that "stars" are the grammatical object of "wipe". But if so, what to do with "appear" in the next line? Is this in parallel with "screw" and "wipe" or does the verb retroactively transform "stars" into its subject? Then in the third line, "screw" reappears, though this time, it would seem as noun, and object of "tighten". And so on. The position of "tighten" at line-end can suggest that it is a pair with "appear" and may even be reflexive, as in "stars appear & tighten [me up]" as against the more likely "tighten screws".

There is another device for the avoidance of "my", which is the use of "the":

> dusk twigs tighten
> slip and whip the skin
> in front of the face (23)

The omission or replacement of pronouns is just one factor here but it is a significant one. There is an unnamed figure in the poem, not referred to in the third person, who is either the one who speaks or is the one spoken to, or is a proxy for both: a personal impersonality. The unspecified character

John Hall

of "you", when it occurs, contributes, I would say, to this effect.

Let me take No. 4 as another case study. The poem moves from indoors in heavy rain, when contact with the outside depends on a functioning aerial, through a strange hinge line, to what must be a journey over fallen snow outside, and with bread to be brought back. This is the second half of the first section:

>   another raindrop starts trickling
>   down the pane then sets off
>   sideways at extraordinary speed
>   to reach the frame
>   & kick back up into the sky

I am about to fillet out the verb-phrases from the first section to highlight the various ways in which movement is both referenced and mimed alongside playful parallelisms and inversions.

>   [...] stops oscillating
>   [...] clearly hear the sweeping
>   up [...]
>
>   hail [...]
>   [...]starts trickling
>   down   [...] then sets off
>   sideways [...]
>   to reach [...]
>   kick back up into [...]

Three lines end in "ing", twice as present progressive and once as gerund ("sweeping"). "ng" is a voiceless continuant ([ŋ]), which has a singing or humming nasal quality, likely to suggest both continuity and a rising pitch. "Stops oscillating" is a play of sibilant, liquid and nasal continuants – s ...s...s...l...ng—and voiceless stops—t...p...t—, with a repeated short o and short i. "[S]tops [...]ing" is paralleled with "starts [...]ing" a few lines later; "...ing / up" with "...ing / down"; the vertical movements of "up" and "down" are "set off" against "sideways" and "back", with an additional play on a difference between "up" and "back up". The last line of the first section in full is "& kick back up into the sky". The "ick" in "kick" has been prepared for in "trickling", but here there is no continuant suffix and there is a decisive set of articulated movements implied in all of

John Hall

"kick", "back", "up" and "into". Try drawing "back up into" as a directional diagram. The voiceless velar stop [*k*] sounds three times in two syllables, and "up" also ends in a voiceless stop.

Towards the end of the poem there is a return to the "up/down" pairing, with "each path leads down as well as up". This is followed with the final three lines:

> but there's only one way to go
>   if you want bread
> oh & bring it back

"If you want bread" has, in this context, a ring of the domestic everyday rather than any grander statement about survival. The poem then ends on another "back". This is very different from ending on an "ing", though phonically it nearly does that too, with "bring" two syllables before. "[G]o" at the end of the third-last line is a long, stressed vowel with no consonant, let alone a stop, to mark its termination. The last line's interjective "oh" recovers some of that force through rhyme and as (I think) reported speech (this is another speaking?).

§

Finding careful prosodic judgements in an analytically slowed-down reading does not mean, necessarily, that these effects were very deliberately planned in; it does mean, though, that there is very careful poetic listening and judgement going on within the composition, and that this has much to do with the wish to keep more than one register in play within every few lines.

§

Behoven 2 is in eight lines, with only 36 syllables in total. Individual lines or even longer passages cannot be usefully excerpted.

> hello
> cuckoo   drunk I
> come through hedges
>   sideways in September twigs
>   flick back and whip you
>   in a list of
>   reasons to be cheerful
>   with asterisks

It is a single movement, in which the strong verbs this time are "flick" and "whip". How deliberately awkward that fourth line is, in applying the mischievous tension, before the flick back. I am reminded of Steve Jonas' *Exercises for Ear* (1968). Like many of the other poems, this too includes an allusion to a familiar song; this time, to Ian Dury's 'Reason to be Cheerful Part 3' (1979), which might in itself import a mood marking, and if it doesn't, then "cheerful / with asterisks" might. *Allegro giocoso?*

The matter of this poem is trivial; its sounding is not. The trivial—what goes on at the T-junction—is as worthy of Hughes' attention as the finest music or painting or food. It is too simple to say that he is a poet of the everyday because for him the everyday is so richly layered. He is clearly interested in improvising poetic frames in which these layers play equally off against each other. This is one task of his prosody.

CITED WORKS

Dury, Ian, & the Blockheads. 1979. 'Reason to be Cheerful Part 3'. London: Stiff Records

Jonas, Steven. 1968. *Exercises for the Ear*. Eltham: Ferry Press

Olson, Charles. 1967. 'Projective Verse' in *Human Universe and Other Essays*, ed. Donald Allen. New York: Grove Press

Schnabel, Artur. 2009. *The Beethoven Piano Sonatas.* Classical Masters

Williams, William Carlos. 1951. *Collected Earlier Poems.* New York: New Directions. (1963).

— *Pictures from Brueghel and other poems.* London: MacGibbon and Kee.

The Summer of Agios Dimitrios: Had Me a Blast

Andrew Bailey

"One gap I did notice," wrote Peter Hughes in an email behind the scenes of this collection, "& was very much hoping someone might touch on, is *The Summer of Agios Dimitrios*." That sounds like evidence for this being, emotionally at least, an important collection to the oeuvre. It's biographically important too, as it details the seven-week holiday that demarcates Peter Hughes, Cambridge education professional snatching time to write, from Peter Hughes, writer and publisher with dependents grown up and gone. The thought of completing forty-nine poems in as many days, the structure of the title sequence, would have been a pleasant aspiration for the former, but attempting it—succeeding at it—feels like part of the initiation into the state of being the latter.

That's all hindsight, of course. The Hughes voice in the final poem offers a less anachronistic reason for the sequence's existence when it writes "I foolishly thought that writing the poem / would make me happier & it did." Judging by the other pleasures studded through the sequence, it's not the only thing that did—sausages, spelunking, saints and the sea are only some of the joys held up in the frame of these daily poems. The way those joys are framed and foregrounded means that it's probably unfair to have started the first quote from the book with an "I", as Hughes more usually prioritises the objects of observation over the observer, as in this more representative quotation:

> four in the morning sea stirring
> on three sides of peninsula
> Orion flat out on mountain top
> too tired & hot to stay in bedroom
> mosquitoes stretching skin of air
> tight like haunted drum in stomach
> outside in a large darkness cool air sets
> with jasmine scent all over the skin […]

(from '2.2 Thursday 20th September')

You can sense the speaker in this—who else's stomach would that be?—but it's interesting to see that it could almost be Orion or the mosquitoes being tired and hot, and that that clause is buried as only one aspect of the world creation here. Similarly the skin is set up to be part of the description of the air. This is related to what Ian Brinton has called the "Orphic immersion" of the sequence[1], bringing to mind the poems of Gary Snyder in which "eating, drinking, reading and looking are all part of a man alive to what there is to be seen and they all act as openings into a world". The speaker being not so much the focus as the lens.

One crude measure of the ratio of self-presentation to outward focus may be taken by counting the uses of "I"—I found twenty-six in the forty-nine poems here, an average barely over half an "I" per poem. Noting that ten uses are concentrated in two poems from the last week should convey a sense of how infrequent that pronoun is through the rest of the sequence. (By way of comparison, I count thirty-six uses of "I" in the forty-one lines of Hugo Williams' 'When I Grow Up', not counting the one in the title.) Of course, it's not a perfect method—for example, by counting "I", I miss "me", but as this is true in both the Hughes sequence and the Williams poem, that's not enough to invalidate it. And method aside, I defy you to deny that it *feels* true.

As pronouns go, there are also several uses of "you", mostly as a casual impersonal pronoun (i.e. a replacement for "one"); it's also pleasant to see there are several uses of "we", as the poet writes to ensure his wife, Lynn, is featured in the work[2]. While in the "unexpectedly complex" tunnels under the peninsula described in '2.6 Monday 24th September' the immersed voice demonstrates both, noting:

> the path you're on is your own
> many of the passages
> are low & narrow the water shallow
> pebbles clear a foot below the surface
> small lights illuminate the route
> the boat rocks if we move
> we duck our heads and proceed feeling
> the roof recede beyond our reach
> a breathtaking sensation
> the world expands until a limestone spur
> cuffs you on the shoulder…

The general "you" on the path here is not the "you" rubbing the bruise from the limestone spur; the latter is a form of "I", if anything, welcoming

---

[1] *Use of English*, volume 61, no. 1, Autumn 2009
[2] She is also the dedicatee of the book, among others, which gives me a warm glow.

a reader into the persona. This is not to suggest, though, that Hughes is wholly self-deleting. His Petrarch versions appearing at the moment[3] seem to have allowed a bit more freedom to put himself forward, as in this extract:

> I don't need all the academic cack
> but I need my Dantes & O'Haras
> my James both Rileys & Ted Berrigan

You can find flashes of that "I" in *The Summer of Agios Dimitrios*, such as the moment in '6.7 Tuesday 23rd October' where "I don't really feel like reading / I feel like watching this / stunning black bee" – but even here that I is rapidly absorbed in attention to the bee's appearance, its "treading & kneading the shining white / bougainvillea flowers". Like good conversation, it's work that is interested in the world outside itself, but with enough self to lend a personality. And like good conversation, it's a very hospitable effect, I find.

It's not an effect restricted to this book, being found before and after. One of the 'Six Klee Paintings' from Hughes' preceding Shearsman collection, *Nistanimera*[4], closes thus:

> you & the landscape stand inside each (other
> & our musty ragged separation stands
> what it can & cans what it must
>
> yes look at the moon) too

and the later Oystercatcher sequence *Behoven*[5] shares its earphones on the Beethoven sonatas with responses such as, from '4', "when the aerial stops oscillating / you clearly hear the sweeping / up of broken plates". It's also not restricted to Hughes—there's a response, for example, to Elaine Randell's *Collected Poems* in the November 2012 issue of *Establishment* in which Steven Waling offers a parallel praise for the way her poems "focus themselves on the object of their concern without any attempt to drag the writer into the picture"[6]. But the immersed, "I"-less voice need not be a pleasure restricted to this sequence, as it is enough for it to be present here, as it clearly is, and for it to communicate so strongly an experience

---

[3] e.g., Peter Hughes, *Regulation Cascade* (Oystercatcher Press, 2012)
[4] Peter Hughes, *Nistanimera* (Shearsman, 2007)
[5] Peter Hughes, *Behoven* (Oystercatcher Press, 2009)
[6] Steven Waling, review of Elaine Randell, *Selected Poems 1970-2006* & *Faulty Mothering* in *Establishment* 2 (November 2012) pp 10-12: http://issuu.com/alecnewman/docs/est_issue_2/11 last accessed 25/11/12

of the place.

It's worth noting where the place is, at this stage. The setting for the sequence is a small fisherman's cottage belonging to Kelvin Corcoran, located on a promontory on the Mani peninsula near the village of Agios Dimitrios, whence the title. The Summer part of the title may seem strange for a sequence set in October and November, but the idiomatic sense of a summer of Agios Dimitrios is that of "Indian Summer" in English, a late warmth in the year, often after a disappointing nominal summer. The summer of 2007 in the Peloponnese had ended with forest fires, which figure in the sequence—"the dark edges of the road / feathered with soot" in '4.6 Monday 8th October', for example.

I went back to old newspapers to verify that fire detail, but the poems are written in a manner which makes me feel a little uncomfortable having done so; they feel so honest to me that I believe in the neighbour, his cat and the accidental collision of the latter with a tuna can in '2.1 Wednesday 19th September', simply from their presence in the poem. Similarly I believe in the date-stamped structure, despite having no explicit evidence that these were completed daily. I say I don't doubt it, but the printed destination of this response meant I felt it was necessary to check—and Hughes assures me by email that "I did decide to write every day & stuck to that". That response is, clearly, just another piece of writing and could equally be mistrusted, but I don't; where would one stop?

Where that sensation of honesty comes from I can only speculate. It can't be the verification above; it feels honest ahead of the checking (although I'm happy it turned out to be so). It may be that we're generally inclined to believe diaries. It may be the opposite of the story in which Auden undercuts Spender's anthology piece by changing the pronoun: "'I think continually of those who were truly great' becomes impossible to take seriously, once the line's first-person pronoun is robbed of its grandeur and pathos by being turned into a domestic diva. 'Your mother thinks continually of those who were truly great' exposes once and for all Spender's 'I' as a posture, as a melodramatic performance."[7] The relative absence of a self-dramatising "I" takes away one of the things you might doubt. It may be related to Hughes' parallel practice as a painter; the objects and characters being placed and presented in the way colour and texture are in the abstract works that cover each Oystercatcher pamphlet, that it's not narrative invention but the placement of what's noticed that fuels the work. It may simply be that there's not a lot here that sounds like the sort

---

[7] as told in several places; here I'm quoting David M Halperin, *How to be Gay* (Harvard University Press, 2012) pp 290-1

of thing you might lie about, or exaggerate—eating tuna and accidentally sending a tin flying is a deeply ordinary experience, and it's no kind of stretch of the imagination to picture next door's cat at the other end of the parabola.

Referring to a deeply ordinary experience is not meant to belittle the work; rather I'd agree with the statement from John James on the reverse of the book, referring to "a measured poetry of the everyday, an intense clarity produced from a steady gaze and replete with respect for the otherness of people, place and things"—although I might quibble with the "measured", which seems to sit oddly with the bursts of energy and enthusiasm that animate parts of this sequence. The choppy energy and short attentions paid to each element of '2.1 Wednesday 19th September' echo the hurried cookery it depicts, and the labyrinthine directions to the elusive St Nicholas in '6.5 Sunday 21st October' could be visualised as being set to Yakety Sax. The measured elements are there alongside them, as when the dream life and real life seem so close in '6.2 Thursday 18th October', and the range of energy between them is one of the pleasures of the sequence. Energy levels in those two poems aside, both involve the sense of "light purposeful steps / & no idea of where to go", as '6.2 Thursday 18th October' has it. Hughes writes that these poems "represent a kind of pause, a release of tension, a wish to be open to what is possible. The most important group of images probably relates to not knowing what is about to happen next!"[8] We can go further than that; not knowing what will happen next means not knowing what's important for those events, what deserves attention and what does not. Hughes' introduction to the Oystercatcher anthology *Sea Pie* includes a key paragraph, one I'm sure will be quoted elsewhere in this collection, that is relevant to this: "I think it's dangerous for poems or presses to have too clear an idea of where they are going. Just around the corner is a place which is different from where you have been. And it's more fun checking out the locals and locale than grumbling about how this is not the same as yesterday and why are there no chips."[9] Without determining where the eyes go in advance, everything has the potential to be an important detail, which allows the everyday in as a source of resonant imagery for the work and influences over the life.

If I'm not over-reaching with that, it has echoes of the "gifted state", as described by Lewis Hyde in *The Gift*:

---

[8] Personal correspondence, November 2012
[9] Peter Hughes (ed.), *Sea Pie* (Shearsman, 2012), p8

In *Biographia Literaria*, Coleridge describes the imagination as "essentially vital" and takes as its hallmark its ability "to shape into one,' an ability he named "the esemplastic power." The imagination has the power to assemble the elements of our experience into coherent, lively wholes: it has a gift.

An artist who wishes to exercise the esemplastic power of the imagination must submit himself to what I shall be calling a "gifted state," one in which he is able to discern the connections inherent in his materials and give the increase, bring the work to life.

[…]

To count, measure, reckon value, or seek the cause of a thing, is to step outside the circle, to cease being "all of a piece" with the flow of gifts and become, instead, one part of the whole reflecting upon another part. We participate in the esemplastic power of a gift by way of a particular kind of unconsciousness, then: unanalytic, undialectical consciousness.[10]

Hughes is open in these poems to a very wide range of materials, such as the discarded "cactus-flavoured ice-cream / refusing to melt in the gutter" of '6.2 Thursday 18 October' that connects, as a metaphor for mistakes, to the butterfly that closes the poem and its place in theories of unpredictability. As with Peter Riley's comment on Hughes' editorial choices, there is "no programmed narrowness"[11] to the content of the poems, either. You need only glance at the page opposite, where the "scraps of rubbish [and] a soft nest of rusty flakes / used to be a dustbin" and provide perhaps the least prepossessing of raw materials, to see this; that glance will also show you that '6.1 Wednesday 17th October' finds its connections worth increasing there, makes a fine example of an esemplastic poiesis, makes a gift from a gifted state. (I am aware of my tendency to wax mystical. In this instance I feel justified by the recording without ridicule of the children's ritual in '1.5 Sunday 16th September'.)

This means I'm finding several versions of generosity here—not only this openness to content, but the hospitality to readers mentioned earlier, not to mention the original generosity in the extended loan of the

---

[10] Lewis Hyde, *The Gift* (Canongate, 2007), pp153-4
[11] http://fortnightlyreview.co.uk/2012/05/hughes-oystercatcher-press/, last accessed 27/11/12

cottage[12]. Generosity being a subject of research in several fields means that you can find, in even a brief bit of web searching, topics such as a 2007 paper[13] on the way an injection of oxytocin increases the propensity for generosity more than one of saline does, a 2011 *Economist* article[14] on mathematical models that demonstrate simulated humans suffer a greater cost for selfishness than for generosity, and an ongoing research group at the University of Notre Dame[15] undertaking cross-humanities study into the subject. The last can be found examining the etymology of the word, sociological aspects and related philosophy, including a definition of Levinas' position on the subject as "an unconditional openness to the Other, an opening of oneself to otherness in a way that is willing to have one's own identity called into question." That feels close enough to the pleasures noted so far to be worth drawing attention to in relation to the work of Hughes, who is clearly a poet overflowing with oxytocin. I am tempted to launch into the etymological side having echoes, with the root "gen", begetting, featuring in the productive nature of this approach, but I have drifted far enough from the work itself, and here I don't have justification in the poems. Rather I am very aware of the final poem's purchase from the airport gift shop, whisky and rather too much chocolate, being a resolutely practical act that should steer me from that temptation.

So, returning to the material of the poems is probably where attention belongs. That last poem figures Norfolk in a bird's eye view that makes serious use of water,

> …with moonlight
> flowing down our rivers past the churches
> schools & hospital blocks to the lighthouse
> poised by the shimmering curves of sea

just as the opening poem notes the county's "oddly-shaped bodies of water" from overhead, which suggests how important an element it is to the sequence, and further poems through the collection that confirm it. '2.5 Sunday 23rd September' serves as an example here, taking place almost entirely at sea. It is partly the narration of a paddle out to sea in a slightly

---

[12] It may also be possible to argue that including 'Physical Geography', nine longer poems that follow the title sequence in the book and share some of its themes, is a further generous act, but I focus on the main section here.
[13] Zak PJ, Stanton AA, Ahmadi S (2007) 'Oxytocin Increases Generosity in Humans.' *PLoS ONE* 2(11): e1128
[14] http://www.economist.com/node/21524698, last accessed 19/11/2012
[15] http://generosityresearch.nd.edu/more-about-the-initiative/, last accessed 19/11/2012

less than airtight dinghy, partly the observation of what is found there. As you'd expect from the earlier material, there's no "I" here – it opens with the activity described phrased as if instructions (or as if phrased in the first person with the pronoun removed), then switches agency between "We paddle", "you swarm", "half the crew abandons ship" and the "unseen lines on my back". Generally these are each a figure of the poet (and wife, in that "we"), but figured so as to step back from the self-presentation, placing the poem in a position of enough self to be interesting and open enough to give the content primacy.

There may be a flavour of Ashbery to the shifting pronouns; there is also pleasure in the shifting referents in a phrasing such as:

> …half the crew abandons ship
> the water facilitated quick descending
> light through clear green pulses
> & waverings onto serrated limestone

where I enjoyed the way the way the water may be facilitating the quick descent of the poet overboard, or of the light – or both, in an *apo koinu* construction, letting the water's facilitation stand in common to the two. There may be another in the "hovering through evening light" which may refer to the viewer or the "indistinct forms" being viewed. Other shifting includes that of the register, between "neglect to placate Poseidon" and "a plastic oar twangs in the air", and the temporal motion between the tenses from the parts happening (Poseidon "hisses underneath as we paddle") and the parts reflected on ("you couldn't tell") before returning to the present ("all forms become indistinct"). The time shift there seems to present the realisation of the previously unknown depths in the water being powerful enough to shift a viewpoint out of the standard timestream, perhaps echoed in the way the creatures hover in evening light while poet's back is patterned by early afternoon sunbeams. That honest openness to what was not known, the willingness to record the fishy depths rather than to report a decided opinion on them, may also be expected from previous discussion.

The fish, the "thin fish with green & purple patterns", that flit through the poem are epiphanic little presences, but the "superglue / scab" that almost repairs the dinghy is more from the tuna-tin and rusted bin end of the imagery spectrum. I enjoy the way the attention flits to the fish from the superglue, via Seferis, limestone and nests of pebbles, holding each up without holding forth on it. The cupboard with which the poem opens is interesting, in that its domestic role seems separate from the rest of the piece, but in being painted blue it prefigures the ocean as a container of things, particularly in the knowledge of Hughes' feeling toward blue: "Blue is the dominant colour I use. Maybe it's the colour of distance, & of the future. You move forward towards it but never inhabit it. The air or water between your fingers is never blue."[16]

We know now, with the success of Oystercatcher and the productivity that may be seen in his expanding bibliography, what inhabited the 2007 writer's future—what came out of the blue, you might say—but the sequence's ability to capture that sense of not knowing, of hanging between what you can't see because it's behind you and the flitting shapes becoming more obscure the further into the blue they are, while sharing the joy of present experience, is a strength worth sharing. It's a sequence important to a generous and gifted writer, on levels including the personal, the historical and literary, and deserves to be read. I could have guessed that reading this poem would make me happier, and it did.

---

[16] Personal correspondence, November 2012

Pulling on the Feathered Leggings

Simon Marsh

In the middle of the night, after dinner in a trattoria on the Tuscolana outskirts of Rome, Hughes suggested we drive to Gran Sasso to watch the sunrise. We took a sizeable piece of pecorino cheese, a bottle of Jameson's, the dog Peg, and set off. We didn't make it to Gran Sasso and slept for a while in the car on the roadside before finally arriving in Viletta Barrea in the Abruzzo National Park around breakfast time and there we spent a couple of days walking in the woods, comparing notes and drafts. Similar episodes in Rome, Milan, Vicenza, Venice and some unremembered locations had preceded the poems of *Bar Magenta*, which was published by John Welch's Many Press in 1988.

Gene Tanta says that "writers who use language as a fluid artefact of the commons help to dislodge static notions of selves". Gene was writing about *The Pistol Tree Poems*, which came out in 2011, but I feel that this was already true back in 1989 when we walked off the previous night's Montepulciano sfuso to the top of that hill in Abruzzo, so that we could experience again and again the thrill of coming out of the trees to gaze at the huge fiery rusting arena of the Camosciara. Come to think of it, it was probably true in 1978, when I first met Peter and when we first started investigating writing poetry together. The writing that we have shared since cannot be separated from our long and extraordinary friendship.

In his brief and refreshingly perky introduction to *Sea Pie*, Peter defines the Oystercatcher poets in the anthology as "individual writers investigating and imagining what is true now". He also says, speaking of the dangers to poetry and poetry publishing of having "too clear an idea of where they are going", that "Just around the corner is a place which is different from where you have been". Peter Hughes has been peeking round that corner for as long as I have known him (occasionally with an upside-down boat on his head). In a recent email he wrote:

> "I've been looking back over the Pistols & pondering on that range of tones & musics. I liked that a lot—the coming round a bend at the end of a line & seeing something totally unexpected. That's what the imagination's FOR bro!"

Peter has ceaselessly encouraged many others to peek, too. Personally, I am grateful to him for having relentlessly nurtured my individual writing projects over the years, and so, not surprisingly, I asked him how he thought I should approach writing this piece. His answer was clear:

> I think the best thing to do with the "Hughes essay" is to be yourself & don't try to make it fit in with your sense of anyone else's agenda. Like those moments in the *Pistol Tree Poems* where quirky mixtures just spring up like in a Sonny Rollins solo. Improv man.

I feel that much, though not all, of the way Peter goes at poetry is in there. The agenda is unmistakably his own, and there is an abiding sense of how the poem, the solo, develops: at times it improvises context, and wells up and flourishes inside that. *Pistol Tree* no.9, starts out with:

> these muggy nights put the mockers on sleep
> stew dream to sweaty clods of nonsense

Then, while groping for his glasses under the bed, the poet finds fireworks instead and blasts his way through the tangibly sax-like tone and phrasing of

> instructions   dusty leakage   dense buff hamstrung jumping jacks
> volcanic cardboard cones   squat tubs of vacant flash and stench

before moving on to free up space to reference other gigs & horns:

> instead I jam along with music for guitar and harp from Mali
> &realize that Frank O'Hara's greatest influence was Louis Armstrong
> straddling that hectic knife-edged urban whirl
> with a lippy rhythmic mastery affecting nonchalance and kites
> but powered by a V8 bolted to the floor under a tablecloth by Miró

The way the poem develops shows how he does not intend to settle for this apparently improvised strangeness. He can equally well use an uncomplicated, accessible tone to deconstruct recognisable riffs and scales: the tune is perhaps familiar, but we'd never heard it played quite that way before:

> …I pull myself back into the present where the drought reveals
> the outlines of another house overlapping our own
> a house that was never built but shows where me might have lived

> a chunk of the house martins' nest just crumbled away
> leaving two chicks dead on the oil-stained drive
> but all the other birds are well & set to fly into the rest of our lives

Pistol No.9 was written in Cambridge, not long before Peter and his wife Lynn made the courageous decision to exchange "income for time" and move to their house in Norfolk. Thirteen years ago, almost to this day, he wrote me letter:

> Actually, there's another address, which is a house we've bought on top of a cliff on the Norfolk coast. It was pretty run-down, with no heating, a dodgy roof, damp, some timber rot and wiring which looked like old spaghetti. But it was cheap! …The idea is that when we retire we… move to Norfolk and go senile to the rhythms of the tides.

Fortunately for all of us, Peter moved sooner than originally planned and decided to set up Oystercatcher instead of going prematurely senile.

In a recent interview, in answer to the question "As a poet, do you always enjoy what you are doing?" Peter replied:

> Writing is a tiny part of being alive. If I don't feel like writing I don't write. I chop up some kindling, prick out some leeks, listen to the cricket or take the dog for a walk. Or read, or plan a trip, or look at some Oystercatcher manuscripts, or update the website. Or make a pasta sauce.

Being alive is a part of writing, too. And this lies at the heart of Peter Hughes' ability to blend and transform. His work is the result of attentive crafting, and an uncommonly complete freeing up of the powers of observation. This very often comes bundled with a simple, uncannily sensitive awareness that is purposefully applied to a ritual blend of day-to-day needs and their whereabouts. In one of the early *Pistol Tree Poems* (number 3), gardening issues abound:

> edging the lawn with worn long-handled shears
> just above sea level   it's hard to understand why maps don't tally
> with what we're walking up and down on
> or why what's in the papers doesn't chime with anyone we know

I would venture to suggest that Hughes is never really *just* "pricking out leeks". The poem continues:

Simon Marsh

> & why of two rhubarb plants
> the first should unfurl and rise like a magic Arabian tent
> all high red poles &voluminous masses of cool green shade
> whispering spices   while the second is barely alive

The Pistol Tree Poems are full of gardening, cooking, house maintenance, and of course, goats. There is a splendid recipe for rhubarb in No.5 and the poem as a whole is a fine example of what Peter means when he says "the process is as important as the product,—where, in fact, the process is the product."

Cambridge: Betty's Gone and the Horse Is Eating Chairs

Often enough, back in 1980 when we were sharing a place in Cambridge, Peter would put on his corduroy jacket, slip a packet of Chesterfield into his pocket, and, as he used to put it, "go for a wander". He was determined, at times restless and misplaced; he believed that walking would somehow or other put things to rights. And it usually did, at least for a while. I walked less, stared at walls more, impatient for tangible evidence of an imminent hopelessness wrapped up in something, tied to a brick, and slung though the bookshop window. I think I can safely say we got on just fine.

Neil Young's stoical, surreal twangy fatalism has accompanied us since our days at The Cambridgeshire College of Arts and Technology (now Anglia University). The "Betty" quote actually comes from a recent amusing e-mail from Peter, but back in our second year at CCAT, we got a band together. Our rig was pretty shoddy: acoustic guitars with cassette recorder microphones blu-tacked to the inside of the guitar body for amplification. The drummer played cardboard box toms and bent, stolen road signs for ride cymbals, but nevertheless, to the chagrin of our musically short-sighted neighbours, we rehearsed unremittingly. We were all English literature undergraduates and so we did try for a while to improvise around our singer's obsession with the idea of setting Samuel Beckett poems to music. However, our best performances were almost always after an evening in the pub, aided by the reverb of the staircase of the house we shared in Vicarage Terrace, playing our version of Neil Young's 'Like a Hurricane' with a hunch-shouldered blues harp solo by Hughes.

More recently, Peter's 'Going for a wander' has led to fine writing such as the *Summer of Agios Dimitrios*, but back in our student days we had to settle for other, makeshift diversions. We once rented the student van to move the belongings of the group's vocalist literally down the road to his new bedsit; a round trip of a couple of miles. How could I possibly know that we would quite literally ditch the van that evening, near the Black Horse pub outside Cambridge after cheerfully trundling around most of East Anglia including the coast. I grew up in Margate and Hughes was extremely worried that my not having seen the sea for some time was doing me harm. We eventually found our way back into town and returned at dawn the next morning with a plastic tank of petrol to recover the vehicle and then explained to the student union why our estimated "use" was off target by several hundred miles.

Three Things

In 1983 after his M.Litt in Modern Poetry in Stirling and around about the time that Peter was doing a hasty TEFL course in Cambridge before moving to L'Aquila, *The Interior Designer's Late Morning* came out. I remember receiving a copy of the book and thinking, yes: being published means fixing things; the chance to move on. I was proud of Peter and felt the need to do the same well-up inside me.

I have learnt three very important things from Peter about poetry. As I said above, publishing, or being published, means fixing your work somehow. It means an end to the tweaking and a chance to turn your attention to something else. The other two things are "the project" and "form". Peter has always said to me that having a project helps the work, helps you focus. Very many, in fact I would say nearly all of his books, are "projects" in this sense. Form helps, too. Not only because it offers a framework, a size of canvas and palette, a range of available notes and scales, but also because it means being able to step outside of that at will. This project and form approach really began to materialise with the *Metro Poems* in 1992 and speaking about that period, Peter said: "For me it was more important to get on with working on a whole sequence of poems, such as the *Metro Poems*, when I lived in Rome, than to fuss about placing a single poem here or there". However, observation and awareness, as well as manifest attentive descriptive choices were already very much in place in Peter's first collection, *The Interior Designer's Late Morning*.

Simon Marsh

The Edge

Sound had seeped into earth
drawn by threads of root silk,
darkening store. It left wet drops and these
the moonlight rung in pure silence.
The moon hardened over Cleeve Hill,
the Ring shadowed itself and night wind
touched a weight of hillside.
Grass blades furled, turned. Hawthorn
blustered once then stilled.
Sky loomed up over the vale where,
some miles away, strands of orange
street lights pointed town towards
the Severn. A single bell wavered
through the wind, shiver of estuary,
of water and thought

This is the earliest of Peter's poems that I am aware of. It was written in the early summer of 1977, on the edge of the Cotswold escarpment, the night before he left Cheltenham to head for the Isles of Scilly where he was to spend the next few months. Those phrases "darkening store" and "touched a weight of hillside" bind everything to a frozen frame, which is at the same time a lengthening of the moment. The way this spills over into what we gather up and take away from the poem has characterised Peter Hughes' best writing ever since. "We are here for the poetry and to preclude the question" neither of us remembers which of us actually came out with that. We were in our twenties and I like to think it was more out of youthful enthusiasm than presumption, while we were sitting in front of another pint of Abbot, tying poems to bricks or hot air balloons.

Rome

One summer evening, it must have been in the '80s, we all drove into town. The idea was to "go for a wander" round Rome, then all meet up later for a lift home. The two of us walked for hours and every so often, actually, as I remember it, very often, we stopped here and there for glass of Ricasoli. It was gone 2 a.m. when Peter decided it might be a good idea to stroll back for the lift, but it was too late: no car, nobody in sight, no lift. At times like these, and at times much worse than these, Peter would take stock and then start a sentence with "The main thing…" In this case, the main thing was to start walking and find a bus. The "main thing" I remember about what followed was the sound of running water; wherever we went there were fountains, gargoyles, the artificial reverb of water trickling underfoot in shallow drains. Peter explained that the city was practically built on water. Even now I remember how his intense and focussed sense of place, of his living the place, had come across then much as it has done with every other place he has lived in since and where I have visited. We eventually found a bus that took us as far as Cinecittà where we arrived at dawn. The rough grain of very first light made me think of that scene in Visconti's *Bellissima* where Anna Magnani rushes her daughter to the studios at sunrise for an audition. We were tracing her steps, the bus left us right there.

As I said earlier, *The Metro Poems* came out in 1992, thanks once again to John Welch. Structurally, the book sums up those two things that Peter has taught me about writing: form and the project. The *Metros* are, in fact, mainly 14-liners. The book doesn't only give you a sense of Rome, or of living in Rome, but of *living* while you are in Rome. In fact, a number of the poems are dedicated to friends, writers and even Art Pepper:

Ottaviano
For Art Pepper

A plush satin bag of tumbly pumice
You could practically hold with your toes.
Under careering petrel and plummeting gannet,
Hiccoughing whales and tamarisk seaweed
Salute unstacked fathoms of departing tide.
Bivalves clap too slowly as mermaids' purses
Roll down the slopes of irregular beds
Through softly abrasive sand and shingle
In restless attempts to succour the alto line.
Unexpended waves lisp along the beaches
To where tangy spit dances on a reed
At the margins of desolate headlands.
Town is a plane tree singing in the night wind
Shadowing the steps to the underground.

The solo is physical space and the task was to render this music with words. What Garry Giddin said about Art Pepper in the *Village Voice* in 1977 might have been written about Ottaviano: "…His present work is

Simon Marsh

alive with splintered tones, modal arpeggios, furious double timing, and acerbic wit. He continues to play from deep inside."

Peter Hughes continues to write from deep inside. This depth provides the stability that makes it possible for him to experiment, improvise and dare:

> in meteoric lines that slit the sky
> wrote notes in dark fecundity
> looming under Cassiopeia
> I invoke the idea of Apollo
>
> I invoke the idea of a poem as
> perpetual enactment of pursuit
> of passion of flight forever turning
> into your damp cavern & formation
>
> Apollo, s'ancor vive il bel desio' (Regulation Cascade)

Piramide: The End of the Line

In the Aaron Game interview, Peter states: "I'd say that my aim is to make up my own line: that is the unit of poetic composition for me." Writing about his painting in the same interview, Peter said that he "worked in layers" and with this in mind I particularly like his cover for Peter Riley's fine Oystercatcher *Best at Night Alone*. The artwork reminds me of the petroglyphs in Vallée des Merveilles or simply of lines on rock that convey a sense of reiteration. There is something lithostratigraphical about Hughes' writing, to the extent that apparently almost free-standing final lines or couplets often result in unexpected hiatus:

> She flicks the light switch but nothing happens.
> I replace the bulb but night keeps falling.
>
> 'Arco di Travertino', from *The Metro Poems*

This is the ripple effect, the poem as locus. I once dropped a pebble off the dam at Lago di Brugneto: I had been told that the more the ripples spread, the deeper the water is. They kept on spreading until I felt a giddy sense of vulnerability, unable to cope with the unfathomableness of the place. There is much of this in the way Hughes' poems often ripple off their own edges:

> We are never going to see the light
> threshed tonight in the courtyards of the stars
>
> 'Marconi', (*The Metro Poems*)

We once visited the Cimitero acattolico near the Piramide of Cestius to pay our respects to Keats and Shelley. We had stuffed our jacket pockets with tiny bottles of Nano Ghiacchiato, a fairly glib white wine, and clinked cautiously past the custodian and on to the graves, where we proposed a solemn toast, actually, a number of toasts. The nearby Porto San Paolo station connects Rome with the coast—the Internet (or a lot of rope) connects the Norfolk coast to the southern tip of Lombardy:

> the fact remains we arrive and will leave
> along a quiet road by a beach at night.
>
> 'Piramide', (*The Metro Poems*)

Why Poetic Collaboration Matters
(A Review of *The Pistol Tree Poems* by Peter Hughes and Simon Marsh)

Gene Tanta

The philosophers have only interpreted the world, in various ways. The point, however, is to change it. —Karl Marx

You must be the change you want to see in the world.
—Mahatma Gandhi

Poets are the unacknowledged legislators of the world.
—Percy Bysshe Shelley

Experimental writers can perform no more politically effective feat toward that noble Marxian goal of changing the world than imaginative collaboration. To the central tenet of the old Left that one must change the world, Gandhi adds that one must be the change one wants to see in the world. By collaborating to create *The Pistol Tree Poems* (Shearsman, 2011), Peter Hughes and Simon Marsh have intervened in the lyric poetry tradition to our benefit.

Whether or not Marx, Gandhi, and Shelley's wisdom resonates with us, today's philosophers (read readers) do not absorb such wisdom by osmosis. Such wisdom needs a shape and language shapes wisdom. Therefore, since language mediates wisdom, a philosophy, in effect, means a love of language. This way, philosophers love wisdom only to the extent to which they love language. A hermit, for instance, knows he is a hermit because of the echolalia of the word hermit which goes bounding inside his head. Along these lines, poets Peter Hughes and Simon Marsh use language for its aesthetic and evocative qualities to make poetry. However, these poems enact the change Hughes and Marsh want to see in the world because the poems are constructed and presented as collaborative. Whatever the medium, collaborative work tempts new subjectivities into being.

Poetic collaboration keeps the selves we think we know in motion.

Such grand framing may be all well and good, but how do poets manage not only to change the world but to be the change they want to see in the world? The process of imaginative collaboration can change the world by changing how we think we know ourselves. We know ourselves, like the hermit in his cave, by how we use language. Writers who use language as a fluid artefact of the commons help to dislodge static notions of selves: Hughes and Marsh make the possible more possible.

Two basic formal constraints score Hughes and Marsh's *The Pistol Tree Poems*, full of that selfsame swirling that goes in and out of egos, places, and senses of craft: Hughes writes the odd poems in the UK, Marsh responds via email from Italy with the even poems. The second constraining factor has each poem end with one line less than the prior poem, thus the collection of 106 poems tapers into silence with the formal whisper of one line from each poet.

> just time to pull on the feathered leggings (Hughes 105)

> & swap love for light (Marsh 106)

Hughes has a gift for the telling chop of idiom while Marsh is an accomplished handler of the heft of figuration. Hughes' boisterous humour is tempered by Marsh's latinate vocabulary and concrete poetry layouts. Thus split, the author-function twains the reader's expectations and the actual reading experience of how she should know the author. Always the twain shall meet.

The following poems show how Hughes and Marsh become the change they wish to see in the world. To be clear, I certainly to not presume to know the writers' political or aesthetical intentions: my claims are those of a reader discussing a text and the function of collaborative writing. Nonetheless, watch and listen to how they perform a shuffling together like a deck of odd and even subject positions, perceptions, local names and concerns:

what to you now are eyes
in nights to come will be stars

         now the pickled onions are fantastic
   a first bite twists the spine 20 degrees
   anti-clockwise with left shoulder dipping
   so folks developed language & language
   developed people which helped us knock through
   but also dumped too much weight in the boot
   thus fucking up most front-wheel drives & those
     who squat in the backs of caves wondering
       what star-light might be like in ideal worlds
     instead of smacking fat pigs with ping-pong
   bats from which the rubber mat flaps free or

> licking Swindon nymphs in the fairy-light
>   lit gloom of St Cecilia's Day where
>   Purcell no it's Mahler is humming you
> mustn't enclose the night inside you you
> you must flood it in eternal light

Norfolk   St. Cecilia's Day 2009 (Hughes 75)

And below I include Marsh's poem sent via email (our contemporary letter-writing medium) in response to Hughes' poem above. These two poems show the call-and-response nature of the collaborative process. Converse to Chevy Chase notions of the lone genius working in his study in a cabin in the woods unmolested by society, these poems suggest the social nature of the creative writing process. After all, being hip means what more than being social? In collaborating to make special objects, Hughes and Marsh perform up to the potential of man as a social animal:

Happy birthday, John Abercrombie

Chipset notes
 Mahler's beamless
   loft of sky
   quietly hewn
     from torrential rain
      & anchored slipshod
        to Earth's off-centred girth
          it's my turn so
           I stare as far as we can
           beyond where the jazz is
           to warm tucks of
            magnetic heat
           coiled round
         hollowed out melodies
   daylight flickers
     and is gone

Varzi   December 2009 (Marsh 76)

Readers will note the place and year of where and when the poem was written left justified under each poem. This information brands each passage with the mortality suggested by the passing of time and space during travel. Some readers may read such branding gestures as claims, however false or true, constructed upon the authority of the local or of the locale. Obviously, this kind of biographical information does situate the word-play in a specific place and time and such placing does invest the poems with that certain auratic glow of having been there. However, essentialism is not a weakness in art: capturing essence is the goal of aesthetics. The essence of places is alluded to throughout the collection with the names of local beaches like Old Hunstanton and local lunch specials like Norfolk Pork & Haddock Chowder.

On the one hand, a collaborative poetry sequence like *The Pistol Tree Poems* implicates readers in the flux of two writers becoming one writer. Moreover, this back and forth between political worldviews and aesthetic sensibilities offers an extended example for the reader of how two poets can work together to become one poet. On the other hand, more conventional lyric poetry with its tacit narrative realism accepts as established fact that market-driven illusion of the subject as a stable and knowable noun. Here, I define more conventional lyric poetry as the poetry of those who own the means of production: those who, because it would lessen their comforts, do not trouble the category of the "I." But what can it mean to punch the Marxian ringtone of "the means of production" in present times, when every desktop PC is a publishing house? How must discussing "the means of production" shift when a playful epistolary dialogue transpires via email between two buddies across Europe? How does an epistolary conversation become a pistol tree conversation? And exactly how much "Jameson's in jam jars" must have been consumed? (Hughes 103)

In *The Pistol Tree Poems* the word "soul" comes up 15 times (on pages 2, 15, 17, 18, and twice on 23, 25, 35, 40, 43, 50, 54, 58, 72, and 78). I bring it up not because I mind the soul metaphor: Emily Dickinson uses it to booming effect. I point to the word "soul" because I want to use it to illustrate how collaborative writing can destabilize the propaganda undergirding a certain kind of subject position.

Can one own the self, mind, or soul (like so many other nouns on the commodity market)? If one can also own the social constructions of the other, the foreigner, or the absent author as part of the free-market of human resources. What if I've been duped into believing that I am I? In other words, what if the I-function is an instance-location in the social fabric of time and space scored into being by the architecture of our habits? With the help of the work of writers like Hughes and Marsh who play with words and with the function of authorship, readers too can be the change they wish to see in the world. For instance, what changes if one thinks of the self, mind, and soul as attributes or qualities pivoting along the continuum of social conventions rather than as commodities to be possessed?

Am I my own property or do I have properties? Am I a piece of property with properties? Simply owning a self, mind, or soul requires no active engagement with the wisdom I receive about these objects or traits. However, weighing the attributes and qualities of a self, mind, or soul demands both critical and creative thinking. If the pre-Socratics, Immanuel Kant, and Jiddu Krishnamurti teach us anything, they teach us that it is bad to think of people as objects. Fine, but what do ethics have to do with two people writing poetry together?

Through its conceptual structure and effects, collaborative poetry inveigles us to consider the shattered and displaced condition of our subjectivities. Through the pleasures and surprises directed by the effects of cutup and syntactic enjambment of units of sound and sense, Hughes and Marsh show readers the aesthetic value that can come from relaxing the ego muscle. Many twentieth-century writers have used the jarring effects of parataxis: from Ezra Pound's adaptation of Chinese and Japanese poetry, to Gertrude Stein and Pablo Picasso's work together, to the canon of experimenters represented in collections such as *Saints of Hysteria: A Half-Century of Collaborative American Poetry*.

To collaborate well as a creative writer, one has to give up the 500 year old idea of the Humanist self as a unique consumer of "the real" as defined by the commodity market from the beginning of European colonial aggression in 1492 up to the email age. This review does nothing new by pointing to the transitory properties of identity. Such a gesture has deep roots all over the world from Greece to Ireland to India as illustrated by the documents of Heraclitian paradox, Socratic doubt, and Romantic poetries. Sometimes these gnarled old roots sprout questions and suggestions as I've tried to outline by discussing the political implications of writing and reading collaborative poetry.

As formal innovation, Hughes and Marsh's collaboration in the form of *The Pistol Tree Poems* entices and challenges readers of contemporary poetry to consider how they themselves could collaborate in order to face their own crises of form in the age of internet, easy travel, and increasing global hardships. How do we readers of the English language, all hermits in the caves of capital, face the freight of our received wisdom?

The Italian Filter

RICCARDO DURANTI

In 'Underground Water', a poem at the end of *The Summer of Agios Dimitrios,* Peter Hughes, while apparently speaking of the water cycle,

> many rocks let water
> through their very being
> others are just riddled with cracks

is actually describing, in what might be construed as one of the most autobiographical passages in his work, the poetic process through which language permeates "lost Cambridge poets".

After many adventures,

> the words will see you
> home before dark
> to feed & water your head
> supporting it at window height
> above the well-stacked dead.

The identification of rock and Peter (via the evangelical pun) rends the metaphoric veil that shrouds the water cycle theme and reveals it as the underground/subconscious method in which the poet filters the words accrued from tradition and usage to hopefully revitalise them and put them to new use.

As a matter of fact that seems to be the spring behind all Hughes' poetic activity: to avoid at all costs the usual—in language, ideas, perspectives. The continuous and marked tension, in his poems, between the everyday and the extraordinary or the extravagant frame around a common subject matter seems to be the hidden engine of his utterances.

Perhaps it is not a far-fetched idea to attribute to this *usualphobic* instinct at least a partial responsibility for his early move to Italy in the '80s. A change of context was needed and Italy provided the necessary medium to reach, at several levels, a desired diversity, a breaking of the mould.

So, after a few tourist trips, in September 1983 Peter lands his first job teaching English as a foreign language in L'Aquila. Next spring he is in Rome where he works for a year, before moving again, this time northwards to Vicenza, for two years. Discounting the difficulties of adapting to the new milieu and the persistence of cultural habits, the influence of this change of background provokes a creative surge in Hughes' poetic output. The enthusiasm for the difference creeps into his poems while his friendship with his former fellow student and co-expatriate to Italy Simon Marsh anchors him in that particular British tradition which they had encountered in Cambridge. From their collaboration comes *Bar Magenta* (1988), the first book they co-authored and named after their favourite meeting point.

In this collection the creative synergy with Simon Marsh comes to the foreground while Italy remains quietly in the background. Daily life, inner and outer, often accompanied by music, goes on and is recorded in minute detail, as in "Milan stretches away like Milan" ('Interval').

'La Madonna di Monte Berico' describes the wonder of waking up next to a NATO airbase in Northern Italy. What stays the same and what seems absurd in such a predicament in daily life: from these dialectics the poet's imagination transmogrifies the Madonna into a war plane, following its flight, "dropping piety, sowing grace."

Less visionary and more visual, 'Christmas morning, L'Aquila' explores the new landscape with the remarkable ability Hughes has of registering the minutest nuances of light and projecting them, along with other sensorial data from his immediate surroundings, onto a cosmological level.

'Train poem' manages instead to transform a trip to Venice in a meta-poetic process in which we can track the growth of a poem (the one we are reading) negotiating the squalid details and sharp corners of common events like a train trip.

Announced by a poem in *Bar Magenta*, 'The Eve of St Cecilia's Day', in 1990 a pamphlet, *Odes on Saint Cecilia's Day,* comes out in Cambridge, but is evidently set in Italy and was in fact written there. The nine poems of the Odes are ushered in by a 'Quintet' forming a tight complex that once again mixes musical strains, existential details and constellations in what we come to recognise as a typical Hughesian mode of composition. Whereas the poems in the 'Quintet' have no recognisable background, right from the start the 'Ode' sets a Roman stage for the graph of the fall from the classical harmony and the power of music as celebrated by

Dryden and Pope to the contemporary dissonance of metropolitan noises recorded by Hughes:

> Baggy old whores topple by in perms,
> dust trickling down the back of the day
>   on a sudden runnel of sweat
> as a slovenly Trastevere afternoon yawns,
> scratches its crotch and listlessly slags off the neighbours.

The sultry atmosphere, mixed with the noise of a bulldozer working on the road, seems to interfere with some mind that would like to concentrate on something else and instead is plunged down in a chthonic dimension with visionary undertones:

> Well below this sour pillow and its load,
> a train smelling of the dead approaches
> a Metro station which has been filled in
> with weeds, lens caps, ketchup, mud and rubble.

Incidentally, this passage is where we can hear the clearest, distorted echo of Dryden's lines, suggesting the power of entropy to re-establish the primeval chaos:

> When Nature underneath a heap
> of jarring atoms lay.

It is interesting to note that this is the first mention of an unidentified and largely symbolical underground station, a forerunner of the cycle of poems that will make up his next collection.

The Roman setting is confirmed in the second poem,

>   …while rusty speakers
> croak out compositions of static and fear.
> An entire day has again gone unrecognized
> in distant rumours of the ring-road,
> a last draughty sun, weeds' shadows lengthening.
> From the direction of the Aventine,
> below the nasal nocturne of the shawm—
> hark! a sackbut, in the Myxolydian mode,
> on a Travertine dunlopillow of 'cellos.

The whole antistrophe of the ode proceeds with its mixed orchestration of noises and music that makes up the sound landscape until the Roman background asserts itself:

> A rower stirs tree reflection,
> sliding down the bloated khaki Tiber.
> Frayed bunting dangles overhead and the stretch
> between the bridges is empty again.

moving from downtown to the southern outskirts of the Eternal City, Hughes draws the poem towards its conclusion modulating light, colours, sounds, moods, images, myths, and realistic details,

> This line is made of air,
> bees browsing dusty chicory and thistle,
> traffic and impulse clotting along the Appia.
> Dead weeds scrape in the breeze
> under power lines that swoop towards Rome.

The Metro Poems (1992) is perhaps the closest to a *Canzoniere* Hughes has written to date, and not only because most poems are crypto-sonnets but because they seem to get organised around a common intent to exhaust the poet's experience in a consistent cycle of poems.

Once again we see the dialectics at work of the natural world superimposed on the sociological background and everyday life, using the transportation system as a skeleton.

The Metro stations coagulate thoughts, perceptions, and daydreams. As if the underground routes were an interface between inner and outer world and provided a structure on which to graft the mental and sensorial experience of the poetic voice, Hughes' descent to the core of the modern world explores in 'Termini', the station where the two lines cross, an Inferno very much like the setting of the *Odes on St. Cecilia's Day*, the depository of the objective correlative of the existential unease coagulating in these poems:

> Shoved by an oppressive, breath-curdling heat
> To a lethargic rummage in the storeroom—
> Dusty unpaired shoes, *Catholicism Today*,
> The cardboard box the fridge came in.
> Next to the two nuclear warheads lie
> The usual inoperable Hoover attachments.

> A ten gallon Kilner jar of pickling vinegar
> Is crammed with a range of the country's pale
> Tasteless regrets, pressing at the glass.
> This all needs chucking out this weekend
> Before we arrive at Termini, get out of
> The Underground and take a proper train
> Through the moving grasses of Etruria
> To wherever our destinations are resolved.

The connection between stations and poems are most of times tenuous, implicit, and elusive. Other times, redundant and misleading (cf. 'Colli Albani' where the station disappears behind the eponymous hills as seen from the poet's house while he sips the white wine that comes from their slopes). But the form is extremely varied: some poems are more focused on the title location than others ('Circo Massimo', 'Piramide') others are just a starting point to propel the narrating voice elsewhere ('Piramide' which evokes Ostia and the sea; 'San Paolo' mysteriously leading to Lake Nemi). Other times, like in 'Marconi', the immediate location sparks an unexpected reference to Pasolini which might stem from the surrounding atmosphere, "Fascist graffiti caress Fascist walls/ at the end of the Infernetto Road", as well as from the book of his poems, perhaps read there.

Each stop is a sort of glass globe portraying moments in the anamorphic and concentrated way Escher engraved so well. And the constant sensitivity of Hughes' painter's eye to the slightest variation in light confirms the optical nature of these oneiric visions. At the end of the book, each globe appears strung on two interlacing threads, and the polysemous "notes" he evokes in 'Subaugusta' ("glistening notes onto these dull peripheries") describe well the way the poet deals with his environment, plucking notes from the air and jotting them down in these poems.

Even after Peter Hughes' return to England in the early '90s, his Italian experience continues to play a role, albeit more indirect, in his poetry. We can find significant Italian connections in the pamphlets published by Equipage in 1995: *Psyche in the Gargano* recalls the setting right in the title poem as well as in another poem, 'Palestrina'. In *Paul Klee's Diary*, the second Equipage pamphlet, there are no direct links to Italy, except as an enthusiasm the poet shares with Klee for Mediterranean culture and light. The two experiences often overlap in the entries of the Diary, and both I's and eyes blend through the same yearnings and memories:

> I have the south in the pit of my stomach
> in the gaps in my skull
> …
>
> I need to be a thousand miles south
>
> …
>
> I eased the edges back
> & stood in the desolation
> of sufficient space
>
> I hear shutters opening
> sense warm olive oil
>   garlic
>   *peperoncini*
> my liver lisping in a pan
> see a brush dancing in a dark kitchen
>
> before a vision of small lights
> stepping down through the night
> to a first glimpse of the Mediterranean
>
> my inner streets awash in the bright
> burn of Ligurian wine
> above the first cool shock
> of clear water under the keel

The dialogue with Italy continues even after a long period of silence, coinciding with the poet's growing concentration on teaching and painting, and resumes in two very original ways. In the autumn of 2006, *Liminal Pleasures* published a special edition of the magazine with several pull-out supplements. One of these was a sequence called *Italia*, in which Hughes revisits all the Italian regions he visited or lived in presenting a sort of semantic map of each *à la Queneau*: notes taken *in situ* or arranged later on the page, like shorthand souvenirs, avoiding syntax as much as possible (perhaps, in order to curb lyrical temptations); yet, the apparently jotted down annotations manage to tell several stories at once, and evoke impressions, feelings and events connected with the place they describe.

                            Umbria

orchard fireflies   supermarket queue   builders merchant

                            silk tie

slit envelope   hilltop enclosure   English mortgage

                          truffle pizza

swallowed guilt   Perugia balcony   rooftop pots

                          disused mill

                        undressed Spoleto
                    drive through the vineyards
                        tune into the reeds
                        row out of earshot
                        feel eel &tench
                       smell sunset water
                           fish stew

ask granddad   remember fennel   check proofs

                          break tooth

The maps all have the same structure (scattered words around a central axis that thickens towards the end before flaring again—sometimes one gets the impression the maps are a little limited by the bi-dimensionality of the page) and present quite a wide range of elements and even a few surprising items. Autobiographical memories of course make up most of the annotations, but the strange typographical rhythm of the compositions manage also to convey a feeling of the peculiarities of each region and the sequence turns out to be an idiosyncratic guide to the country.

The Pistol Tree Poems, published by Shearsman in 2011, witness the persistence of the poet's exchange with his friend Simon Marsh, who continued to live in Italy. They exchange back and forth poetical messages from May 2006 to June 2010, sharing inside jokes, myths and private codes, comments on their everyday life and memories. The result is a sort of parallel Zibaldone recording everything from food and wine experiences to references to landscape, music, politics and literature. It is interesting to note, for our purposes, that at least once, walking down memory lane, Hughes recalls his first trip to Italy and we get a first-hand report of his adventures in Italy in his youthful days:

so after 3 days throwing up in Siracusa (water poisoning - Midsummer 1980)
    I catch the night-train to Agrigento   [Dorian]
      carrying less weight & with another page bleached clean in my head
        I arrive after the last bar has closed
          & wander southwards from the city
            until I find a broken orchard wall:
              & slept on Earth   too near a goat   & manger full of stars
I awoke to the silhouette of a dog facing east   & sitting next to my head
   stirring when I stirred   but with a dogged calm
    we shared Parmesan rind & stale soft crackers in the dark
      as another dog ghosted in under the trees   & then another
        & we set off to reach the temples by dawn with a pack of 20 happy
            hounds…

we arrived before first light   the Temple of Concord   or Demeter…
   temples remade by changing light in an air   which held wild thyme
    in years of breeze from off the sea   I looked over my own shoulder
      & although my view was overseen   I saw enough
       to leave a sense of rising *small boats lifted on a long swell*   forever in my head…

Progressively shorter, the poetic epistles cover with humour and pathos much of the common ground of their collaboration and friendship as witnessed by periodical references to their meetings in Bar Magenta.

    One thing remains to be said about Hughes' relationship with Italian culture. Throughout his creative life, an iconoclastic attitude emerges with some regularity. One only needs to examine his non-translations from Petrarch to understand this peculiar trait in his poetry. Reportedly, the *Canzoniere* was the first book Hughes bought in L'Aquila in 1983 and, in spite of the fact that his Italian is excellent, over the years he proceeded to issue versions of the *sonetti* which programmatically veer widely from the original content, keeping with it only the slightest rhythmic connection as we can easily verify when we put them side by side (see below). Thus the amorous or civil inspiration of the early Italian poet is systematically substituted by humorous contemporary references (Procol Harum's lyrics and other incongruous autobiographical or nonsensical material) whose intent is, paradoxically, to put as much distance as possible (instead of reducing it) between the original and the modern "version" in order to emphasise the gap between the two worlds and their different expressive attitudes.

Sonetto CXXIII (Bortoli, XCVIII)

Quel vago impallidir che 'l dolce riso
d'un'amorosa nebbia ricoperse,
con tanta maiestade al cor s'offerse
che li si fece incontr'a mezzo 'l viso.

Conobbi allor sí come in paradiso
vede l'un l'altro, in tal guisa s'aperse
quel pietoso penser ch'altri non scerse:
ma vidil' io, ch'altrove non m'affiso.

Ogni angelica vista, ogni atto humile
che già mai in donna ov'amor fosse apparve,
fôra uno sdegno a lato a quel ch'i' dico.

Chinava a terra il bel guardo gentile,
et tacendo dicea, come a me parve:
Chi m'allontana il mio fedele amico?

Petrarch 98

all the poetic snowclone detritus
sprinkles the jellymould anthologies
& chilled creative writing nurseries
in which silence is golden gets knocked off

the top of the charts by a whiter shade
of pale followed by all you need is love
are one thing but this is an obsession
so I'm fracking the remaining content

in the wrecked deconsecrated chambers
& such privatised workings of the heart
boarded up & out of bounds until spring

& inspiration shake hands with the means
of production values pedestrian
malls & precincts baby it's cold outside

* * *

Riccardo Duranti

This bird's eye survey of Peter Hughes' relationship with Italian culture does not pretend to exhaust the theme of the impact that living and working in Italy for several years has had on his development as a poet. Rather it seeks to locate and fix a few landmarks as they emerge from an examination of his poetical work so far. Hopefully, more cues may emerge in this as in other contexts, for example it would be interesting to investigate the influence that Italian landscape and art have had on his parallel career as a painter. Our personal surmise is that the results would not vary that much. But this is material for another study.

"dust on the tongues of strangers like us": Peter Hughes' Petrarch

Simon Howard

In one sense the question "what is a sonnet?" is easy enough to answer. It's a poem in 14 lines, the form originating "almost certainly at the Sicilian court of Emperor Frederick II (1194-1250) … and its originator there was—again almost certainly—an administrative notary from Apulia named Giacomo da Lentini (*fl.* 1220-40)."[1] It bears, at origin, traces of other forms and models and rhetorics, some of local origin, others—implying issues of cultural appropriation and prestige—cosmopolitan, most importantly those derived from Provençal Troubadour poetry (Ezra Pound claimed the sonnet resulted "when some chap got stuck in the effort to make a canzone." This is almost certainly not correct).[2] It is also a plural a, in that various rhyming schemes are deployed in various sonnet types (though there are variants and mutations and the identification of competing "traditions" is wildly over schematic) as are differing stanzaic divisions. Until the twentieth century, that is, when the charm of rhyme in particular—again with exceptions—is worn away by the erosive (in)action of accumulative banalities and where the observation of rhyme and other traditional "schemes"—rhythmic (in Anglophone literature, iambic pentameter in particular) and shaping—is viewed as redundant / external / formulaic constraint, at least to those modernist and postmodernist poetries and poetics dedicated to exploring the deconstruction and / or mutation / annihilation of form. (Of form, perhaps, rather than genre, the latter being an idea which stages a return in literary theory and criticism predominantly of pre and early modern literatures, with parallel explorations in Oulipian writing and the postmodern novel, with their quasi-masochistic / parodic play involving constraint and artifice).

Peter Hughes' Petrarch sonnets don't rhyme, but they do show an involvement with Petrarch's stanzaic structures and more widely with the

---

[1] William J. Kennedy, 'European beginnings and transmissions: Dante, Petrarch and the sonnet sequence.' In *The Cambridge Companion to the Sonnet*, ed. A. D. Cousins and Peter Howarth, Cambridge University Press 2011, p. 84.
[2] Ezra Pound, 'Cavalcanti.' In *The Literary Essays of Ezra Pound*, ed. T. S. Eliot, Faber and Faber, 1985, quoted by Jeff Hilson, introduction to *The Reality Street Book of Sonnets*, Reality Street Editions 2008, p.14.

rhetorical framework of the sonnets versioned (while also, in their fast-ish & loose-ish adherence to decasyllables, invoking earlier Anglophone sonneteering) and in so doing they make intimate advances towards and contacts with Petrarch's texts that create a version of trans-form-u-lation foregrounding intimacy, estrangement, transgression, fidelity, betrayal, proximity, immeasurable distance, in a way that, I'd argue, enacts a mimesis or shapes a mirror-echo of what I identify as Hughes' Petrarchs' overarching concerns:

i) love as repetition in difference and as repetition in despite of indifference (perseverance: see also v)

ii) love as supplement, a supplement to something named as "life" in the context of day-to-day living, where emotion and emotional simulacra, where emancipation and capitalism, appear to be in one-way-street supplement-as-substitute in continual subtractive / surplus exchanges: in the sonnet after 'Già fiammeggiava l'amorosa stella', "soapy cover versions sanitize an / edginess that used to keep us on our / toes …/ & nothing is as I remembered it / for example Gordon is a Mormon"[3]; a supplement that potentially moves in a contrary direction to that one-way-street (offends against the one-way system), and yet the fear is also, under a nihilistic star (for what are the cover versions about, if not LOVE—even "Gordon is a Mormon"?), a deludedly (and deludingly) complicit one—in the sonnet after 'Benedetto sia 'l giorno, et 'l mese et l'anno'):

& what do you think about these love songs
imagined passion meeting displaced lit-fest
moves alongside love that stands for life [4]
(et benedette sian tutte le carte / ov'io fama l'acquisto, e 'l pensier

---

[3] From Peter Hughes, *Quite Frankly: After Petrarch Canzoniere 1 – 28*, Like This Press 2013. "Gordon is a Mormon" refers to Jilted John's (aka Graham Fellows) hit single of 1978, 'Gordon is a Moron': "I've been going out with a girl / Her name is Julie / But last night she said to me / When we were watching telly / (this is what she said) / She said 'listen John I love you / But there's this bloke I fancy / I don't want to two time you / So it's the end for you and me'/ … / I was so upset that I cried all the way to the chip shop / When I came out there was Gordon standing at the bus stop / And guess who was with him / Yeah, Julie, and they were both laughing at me / Oh, she is cruel and heartless / To pack me for Gordon / Just cos he's better looking than me / Just cos he's cool and trendy / But I know he's a moron, Gordon is a moron / Gordon is a moron, Gordon is a moron…"
[4] Forthcoming, 2013.

Simon Howard

mio / ch'è sol di lei sì ch'altra non v'à parte" / "and blessed be all the pages where I gain fame for her, and my thoughts, which are only of her, so that no other has part in them!"[5]

where "love" dis(mis?)places life as referent, becomes an uncannily object-like signifier; and yet in that it "stands for life" (with a bawdy pun sticking its ... tongue out) "it' also stands up *for* life (and somehow the loved other returns as a kind of obstinate resistance to poetic idealisation as commodification / to being turned into something like a mirroring thing, returns via a textual redaction or graffiti-ing over of Petrarch's hyperbolically demonstrative insistence that his thoughts are fixed and single in purpose, and his text (his physical text, "tutte le carte")... devoted in intent, to render itself ostentatiously transparent in the pursuit of fame for "her" (a pursuit ending, of course, in fame or the laurels for him)

iii) place and being out of place

(iv) time and being out of time (the coinciding within certain of Petrarch's sonnets of satire on the Papal Court at Avignon, his grief at Italy's fragmentation and his own exilic status, and discourses of love, and the disjunctive, jarring, collision / collusion of those coincidings with Hughes's satire of spectacular and specular warfare, of commodification / globalisation, and the invisibility—sharply contrasting with but drawing on Petrarch's reference to the Ovidian metamorphosis of Daphne into a laurel bush to escape Apollo the god of poetry's sexual advances and Petrarch's, fleetingly, triumphalist association of Laura with the poetic laurels—of being a poet in love in a supermarket car park or at a car boot sale or of a poet being anything at all in a world where being is defined by waged work and where education has been redefined as induction for the ((world of)) work)

(v) the persistence of an I behind or among the staged "I" of the lyric voice, the obstinate matter of the fact-ness of the loving subject outside the poem yet inside the poem (and sometimes

---

[5] Quotations from Petrarch and English prose translations are from *Petrarch's Lyric Poems: The Rime sparse and Other Lyrics*, trans. and ed. Robert M. Durling, Harvard University Press, 1976.

bewildered at finding itself there) and consequentially the enduring independence from the poem and the poet of the object of the lover's love.

These concerns, I suggest, place Peter Hughes' Petrarch poems in richly productive critical relations, contacts, situations, relevant to Petrarch's work (and subsequent Petrarch inspired work, crucially that of the Elizabethan sonneteers) and to how linguistically innovative poetry (the a-tradition Hughes' poetry and editorial work nomadically inhabits) has (re-) engaged with the sonnet (so peremptorily dismissed by modernist Pound near the beginning of the last century) over the past 50 or so years (roughly—very roughly—from Ted Berrigan's celebrated sonnets onwards: "I need my Dantes & O'Haras / my James both Rileys & Ted Berrigan"[6]).

So that when Hughes' sonnet after 'Più di me lieta non si vede a terra' speaks of a "you" that in Petrarch is a fellow poet who has turned his back on love and becomes in the penultimate stanza a specialist collective ("Et tutti voi ch'Amor laudate in rima" / "And all you who praise love in Rhyme"), the effect is multiply and perplexingly intimate, familiar and personal yet also wanderingly intra-subjective: the reference indeterminate enough for the you to be I conversing with "I"; for it to summon an untimely contemporaneity of Petrarch as poet, lover and meta-poet (not timeless, but time-travelling); and for it to be the linguistically innovative poet dreaming of starting a riot with words only to find that riot going on around her / him … a riot evincing not the slightest recognition of any authorial provenance or authority whatsoever (the homely ricketiness of the milk-float and the "you"'s new found buoyancy beautifully, wittily, deturning, de- and re-inflating Petrarch's nautical simile: "Piú di me lieta non si vede a terra / nave da l'onde combattuta et vinta / quando la gente di pietà depinta / su per la riva a ringraziar s'atterra" / "More glad than I, was never ship come to land after being battled and conquered by the waves, when its people, showing devotion to their colour, kneel on the shore to give thanks"). And for the poem to be a version / a translation-transformation, of the modernist imperative to "make it new" within a context of nomadic, polyphonic, restlessness (the "rinsed clean" both continuing the deturning of Petrarch's seafaring discourse and bringing to mind the cleansing of the sun of metaphor—by way of metaphor, naturally

---

[6] After 'S'amore o morte non dà qualque stroppio' in *Regulation Cascade*, Oystercatcher Press, 2012.

as it were—in Wallace Stevens' 'Notes Toward a Supreme Fiction' … with "meteors" punning on metaphors):

> no milk-float trundling through the aftermath
> of last summer's riots ever made it
> back to the depot with greater relief
> than I feel in your new buoyancy
>
> like a prisoner on death-row hearing word
> of some inexplicable reprieve
> you seem to walk back out into the world
> shrugging off the shackles of convention
>
> rinsed clean of others' expectations
> & left with no attachment to the past
> you come back to language like a stranger
>
> attend to these meteors & apples
> water trickling through an old garden hose
> to resurrect the body of your mind[7]

Before close reading one of Peter Hughes' Petrarchs against the general background of the "overarching concerns" I've sketched above, and with an eye to the formal effects and affects of those concerns, I want to make some observations about Petrarch and scatteredness / Hughes and scatteredness, and about the notion of a separable lyric "I" and the perplexed yet obstinately enduring (in multiple significations) I in Hughes' Petrarchs, drawing on an essay by Teodolinda Barolini for Petrarch and a book by Catherine Bates for the lyric "I" separation.[8]

In a note prefatory to *Regulation Cascade* Hughes writes: "Petrarch wrote over three hundred sonnets & the following are English versions of what have become known, in my head, as The Second Batch. This group consists of his sonnets 27–46." In fact Petrarch wrote 317 sonnets, together with 29 canzoni, 9 sestinas, 4 madrigals and 7 ballate, collected and ordered by Petrarch himself under the title *Rime sparse* or *Scattered rhymes* (though originally with a Latin title, *Rerum vulgarium fragmenta* or *Fragments written in the vernacular*: bringing into relief the vernacular

---
[7] *Quite Frankly*.
[8] Teodolinda Barolini, 'The Self in the Labyrinth of Time (*Rerum vulgarium fragmenta*)' in *Petrarch: A Critical Guide to the Complete Works*, ed. Victoria Kirkham & Armando Maggi, University of Chicago Press, 2009; Catherine Bates, *Masculinity, Gender and Identity in the English Renaissance Lyric*, Cambridge University Press, 2007.

/ Latin argument proposed by Dante in *De vulgari eloquentia* whose own Latin title stages the case for the vernacular via parergonal paradox). I'd suggest that a sense of the vernacular as expressively freer than, in this case, a certain received poetic diction (standing in for the "atemporal" elevation of Latin) as richer and yet simultaneously absurd(ist) and malapropistic through use's abuses is present in lines like Peter Hughes's throwaway "Gordon is a Mormon" or the wonderfully precise descent from historical high to anecdotal low in "I blame the Albigensian crusade / & certain adolescent accidents" (after 'Quella fenestra ove l'un sol si verde').[9]

In terms of complexity of authorial / editorial ordering and collective structure Petrarch's *Rime sparse* is unprecedented as a work bringing together—pre-announced as scattered—lyric poems, Dante's *La vita nuova* being greatly more compressed in terms of number of poems and time span of composition with the poems interspersing a prose narrative, and other earlier collections resulting from scribal / editorial decisions (fascinating as those certainly are) not authorial shaping. The span of compositional time, and the evidences of an evolving / ordering structure, taken together are remarkable: "He apparently began writing the poems that were to form the *Rime sparse* in the early 1330s; perhaps by 1335 he had decided to make a collection; by the mid-1350s most of the 366 poems had been drafted … The *Rime sparse* are arranged *as if* they are in a chronological order, and most modern opinion holds that they are in fact more or less, and with certain notable exceptions, in the order of composition. But this cannot be determined with much reliability, since the anniversary poems, which used to be thought of as anchors of a "real" chronology, could have been written years later or even years earlier … The work presents a *fictional* chronology that should not be confused with a real one, and the ordering of the poems derives from artistic principles."[10] Petrarch's note, written in a copy of Virgil, recording Laura's death, seems personal indeed[11], but the reality of Laura before, as it were, poetic idealisation, has long been

---

[9] From Peter Hughes, *Soft Rush*, The Red Ceilings Press, 2013.
[10] Durling, op. cit., introduction p. 12.
[11] "Laura, illustrious by her virtues, and long celebrated in my songs, first greeted my eyes in the days of my youth, the 6th of April, 1327, at Avignon; and in the same city, at the same hour of the same 6th of April, but in the year 1348, withdrew from life, while I was at Verona, unconscious of my loss…. Her chaste and lovely body was interred on the evening of the same day in the church of the Minorites: her soul, as I believe, returned to heaven, whence it came. To write these lines in bitter memory of this event, and in the place where they will most often meet my eyes, has in it something of a cruel sweetness, but I forget that nothing more ought in this life to please me." http://www.brown.edu/Departments/Italian_Studies/dweb/plague/perspectives/petrarca.php

disputed (that she was an ancestor of the Marquis de Sade has a certain rightness on each Augustinian level of meaning, the literal, the allegorical, the moral, and the eschatological),[12] but a division of the *Rime sparse* into poems written before and after that event, rather than as so arranged to represent a before and after that event, is not backed up by philological evidence. Poem and event do not coincide / poems are untimely as well as (in the familiar conceit) monuments against time. But it's the idea of fragmentation set alongside as well as within a volume Petrarch took such pains to arrange (though they form nothing like the major part of his life's work, "some 10,000 lines of Italian verse ... as opposed to thousands of pages of verse and prose in Latin")[13] that interests me, both in terms of Hughes' idea of his versions as batches, and Hughes' zooming in on fragmentation and dispersal.

> "From what we know of Petrarch's life as a writer we can get some sense of an inner life more horizontal than vertical, more committed to making multiple connections among the many morphing *lauri* in the one *selva* than to moving from one integral *lauro* to an utterly discrete something else.
> At the same time the fragmentariness of some of the *labores* only adds to the sense of their all ultimately belonging to one overarching life—one authored and authorized self—which, one *racolto*, once etymologically perfected through death and hindsight, is in fact strangely cohesive and complete."[14]

Catherine Bate, in her book *Masculinity, Gender and Identity in the English Renaissance Lyric* constructs an argument which in many ways is at odds with Barolini's concept of an overarching life, having to do with dispersal, scattering of identity, metamorphoses that undo ideas of stability of identity and / as gender. But her argument against New Historicist readings of the "I" in Renaissance lyric poetry, which she refers back to similar claims concerning Petrarch as originator of the tradition and to suggestions that, more knowingly than Petrarch, with greater theoretical consistency, Wyatt and the Elizabethans understood the poetic "I" as artificial construct, as an element in a game of power, seems to me relevant to Hughes' refusal to absolve the I of the "I", or to see the latter as a sign of the absence of the former, and to connect with Hughes' laconic refusal of organised

---

[12] http://en.wikipedia.org/wiki/Laura_de_Noves. For "levels" of interpretation see St. Augustin, *De doctrina christiana*.
[13] Durling, op. cit., introduction p. 7.
[14] Barolini, op. cit. p. 57.

Simon Howard

scatteredness in his "batch" remark. For Bates, to read the lyric "I" of Elizabethan poetry (and by extension any lyric "I") as a separable construct is merely to consolidate the identity and singularity of the authorial (and by implication and identification critical) self. So that the author stands securely separate from the abjection, the powerlessness, the masochism and perversities of the purportedly theatrical I who speaks in the poems. Selfhood (and masculinity and femininity as uncomplicated categories distinct and apart) are preserved in the poet's life even as they are disclaimed for the self who "lives" in the poem. The poet's skill in performing this trick wins the poet praise and augments the poet's power and prestige as authorial self. The I / "I" relation is a recuperative power relation. Bates, by contrast, suggests we take what the poem's voice(r)s say seriously; that we read their bodily and psychological self-dismantlings as continuous with all selfhood's scattering and undoing by language /s. Which brings me back to Peter Hughes' Petrarch.

Sonnet 11 from *Regulation Cascade* is a version of Petrarch's "Il mio adversario in cui veder solete', a poem which elaborately multiplies and metamorphoses mirrors: Laura, seeing herself beauteous in her mirror (personified as Petrarch's adversary, mirroring back that which makes him in the eyes of the one mirrored—where, without the mirror, he was himself mirrored—insignificant) rejects Petrarch following the mirror's counsel: "Per consiglio di lui, donna, m'avete / scacciato del mio dolce albergo fora: / misero esilio! avegna ch'i' non fora / d'abitar degno ove voi sola siete" / "By his counsel, Lady, you have driven me out of my sweet dwelling: miserable exile! even though I may not be worthy to dwell where you are alone." Things become more complicated, more meta-mirrored, with the Ovidian invocation in the closing tercet of Narcissus:

> Certo, se vi rimembra di Narcisso,
> questo et quel corso ad un termino vanno—
> benché di sì bel fior sia indegna l'erba.

("Certainly if you remember Narcissus, this and that course lead to one goal—although the grass is unworthy of so lovely a flower"). If Petrarch is accusing Laura of being like Narcissus then he has previously deconstructed that identification by wishing to be in the place of the mirror, Laura-eyed, in the situation of Narcissus's self-adoring gaze: "Ma s'io v'era saldi chiovi fisso / non devea specchio farvi per mio danno / a voi stessa piacendo aspra et superba" / "But if I had been nailed there firmly, a mirror should not have made you, because you pleased yourself, harsh and proud to my harm." Identity and gender drift, unstable, intermingling – who is Narcissus, Laura or the lyric I / Petrarch? And the masochism, the unworthiness, of the lover metamorphoses into sadism; driving nails into Laura's eyes. And a strange temporal compression occurs: Narcissus becomes a flower (Laura?) without drowning and the grass surrounding Laura (a plural setting) the unworthy… Petrarch?

Here is Peter Hughes' poem:

>after I'd invented mountaineering
>& then the dark ages I decided
>I'd try my hand at making up the self
>ready for the rise of the bourgeoisie
>
>first stare at an image in a mirror
>become entangled in bright absences
>banished to flatpack oblivion
>at the back of some suburban warehouse
>
>you add label after label until
>you've made a 3D papier-mâché
>robot programmed by the Murdochs
>
>then you end up addicted to updates
>each vacancy replacing another
>as your blood turns slowly into water

The invention of mountaineering refers to Petrarch's letter, written around 1350, concerning his ascent of Mont Ventoux on April 26, 1336 (note, again, the significant gap in time between event and text)[15]. Petrarch claims to have been the first person since antiquity to have climbed a mountain for the sake of the view alone. The text has often been cited to indicate a shift from something called the Medieval to something called the Renaissance Humanist mind, and that kind of simplistic approach is neatly parodied in Hughes' invention of mountaineering. But running with and against Petrarch's poem (as though removing the distracting light of Laura's reflected and reflecting eyes to show the self-promotion in bare daylight) the boasts keep coming, comically and insouciantly; the

---

[15] For a text of the Mont Ventoux letter, see http://www.fordham.edu/halsall/source/petrarch-ventoux.asp

Simon Howard

invention of selfhood brings to the surface issues concerning the self and the poetic self in Petrarch that reach back to Ovid and forward to the question of self-reflexiveness and the critical tradition concerning that supposed self-reflexiveness Bates deconstructs in the context of Elizabethan sonnet sequences.

Things turn … darker, and Petrarch begins to recede with "ready for the rise of the bourgeoisie." And yet Petrarch's sonnet comes closer, for now the (Ovidian / Narcissistic) mirror arrives. Simultaneously the first person voice ghosts away, to be replaced by impersonal "instructions for use" addressed to … us? the poet's self? the absent Laura / beloved?: "first stare at an image in a mirror / become entangled in bright absences." Hughes' poems certainly stand alone and need not be read alongside their Petrarchan doubles. Similarly, they stand to be read alongside their Petrarchan doubles as a mode of reading (in that they engage with Petrarch's sonnets, are steeped in the shape and discursive contours of those sonnets) and the reading isn't one way; as in Mieke Bal's discussions of quotation and intertextuality in contemporary "baroque" art and Caravaggio so the illuminations work both ways, both texts experience transformation.[16] The "bright absences" (by a negative route) illuminate the sadistic act of blinding of Laura that occurs within Petrarch's text. And love makes an appearance, touchingly so, with those "bright absences," an inventive and loving version of Petrarchan paradox so (be)loved of Elizabethan sonneteers.

Now it's banishment, exile (there's a further complexity in Petrarch's text in that his banishment from Florence and his exilic presence in Provence, attached to the court of the Avignon popes, allowed him to first see Laura and therefore experience the banishment / exile from her eyes recorded in the poem). Significantly (I believe) absent from Hughes' Petrarch is the topography of Italy (where Petrarch was to return, but wherein—the country scattered, dismembered and strife and faction riven—Petrarch also felt internally in exile). In *The Metro Poems* (1992) Hughes records in richly and often phantasmagorically sensuous detail his impressions of Italian cities and locations visited ("Through dark branches of pathside hornbeam / a hundred golden persimmon beat / on a slope of dusk and hillside wind")[17] and Italy (and Greece) are recurring locations in Hughes's work. Scarcely at all in the Petrarchs, though. Rather, as though

---

[16] Mieke Bal, *Quoting Caravaggio: Contemporary Art, Preposterous History*, University of Chicago Press, 2001.

[17] Peter Hughes, 'Ponte Lungo' from *The Metro Poems* in *Blueroads: Selected Poems*, Salt Publishing, 2003.

registering banishment from poetically evocable landscapes, "banished to flatpack oblivion / at the back of some suburban warehouse."

The externality of Laura that baffles and provokes the desire for (of) interiority in Petrarch becomes a nightmare of media programmed robotic vacuity ("programmed by the Murdochs"), of an addiction that rhymes *against* the addiction of erotic and emotional attachment ("addicted to updates"); metamorphoses—phenomena of strange though terrible beauty—becoming mechanical "replacements"

> as your blood turns slowly into water

By this stage any semblance of stability in identifying who is speaking to who, or of a coherent subjectivity presiding over the subjective disintegrations of lyric selfhood, has … turned to water; fleeting, evanescent, and on average 57% of any human animal's body weight. Yet this transformation re-evokes the Narcissus story, where in Petrarch the moment of drowning was hidden. And, suddenly, a kind of transformative magic reasserts itself. This *is* a wonder, and it is a wonder worked by love (that strange sensation when you catch sight of or are exhilaratedly with someone you love where … your blood seems slowly to be turning to water). The Murdochs are plural yet corporate; the individual is disparate yet unique, residual yet resilient. As a as yet unpublished Hughes' Petrarch puts it:

> in poetry meetings I guess the clerks
> are talking about the death of the I
> can't help it if I'm still in love with you
>   (after 'Fiamma dal ciel su le tue treccie piova')
>
> under the massive and still frost free
> scintillation of pierced stars
>
> the dog sits in a mild October gale
> under the energised band of the milky way
> demented with night
> unwilling to come back
> into the caravan[18]

"Il n'y a pas de hors-texte," in Derrida's famous, infamous, notable, notorious and eerily illegible formulation from *De la grammatologie*[19]. Eerily illegible, because it erases itself in inscription, in internal transmission so to

---
[18] Peter Hughes, 'Peg' from *Nistanimera*, Shearsman Books, 2007.

[19] Les Éditions de minuit, 1967.

… write, and has certainly undergone erasure in translation and Chinese whispers based on translation: because "il n'y a pas de hors-texte" does not equate to "everything is text," or "there's nothing outside the text / texts." Rather, what there isn't is a / the hors-texte, which is a rather different idea. And, outside, the dog sits, under the energised, unreadable, inscrutable, constantly scrutinised, continually anxiously read for anything from clues to the future, signs of the presence of God, the presence of Xorgs from the planet Xarg, as to whether he loves me or she loves whoever, "demented with night." De-meant-ed? An overload of signification, a text which is *nothing but outside*, and where being unwilling to come back into the caravan is, perhaps, being unwilling to exit poetic madness ("The lunatic, the lover, and the poet / Are of imagination all compact. / One sees more devils than vast hell can hold— / That is the madman. The lover, all as frantic, / Sees Helen's beauty in a brow of Egypt. / The poet's eye, in fine frenzy rolling, / Doth glance from heaven to Earth, from Earth to heaven. / And as imagination bodies forth / The forms of things unknown, the poet's pen / Turns them to shapes and gives to airy nothing / A local habitation and a name.").[20] (Sartre, in *L'idiot de la famille*, reads Flaubert's "mot juste" as a kind of muteness, an exteriority to a signifier's connection to a signified: Flaubert is like a dog, Sartre writes, who knows when people in a room are talking about him but can't make the signifiers into signifieds and so in his anxiety acts the fool, dashing about the room, frantically wagging his tale and knocking into the furniture.)[21]

I'll conclude this essay with a close reading of one of Peter Hughes' Petrarchs, against the background of the issues I've previously sketched out: emotional and physical dislocation, the persistence as and as not-text of the self that cannot simply, recuperatively, be ironised as an "I", with an author standing knowingly behind that "I" (so that the deconstruction of the cogito, so often thought of as a denial of all forms of identity becomes a celebration of identity scattered, plural, but also interconnected: enmeshed in networks of poetic transmission—in this instance, Hughes's engagement with Petrarch—connected to other /s by love and persistence through and against the turned away face of love, at defiant unease in a militarised / commodified / globalised / Murdochised world, whose invasive, incorporating, engorging network and net-working is perhaps what the "hors-texte" irreally looks like). I'll allow Petrarch to fade into the background, and read the poem without specific reference to that particular double.

---

[20] William Shakespeare, *A Midsummer Night's Dream*, V.I, ll. 7-17.
[21] *L'idiot de la famille : Gustave Flaubert de 1821 à 1857*, Gallimard, 1971-1972, 3 volumes.

The poem is from *Soft Rush*:

> just before dawn & the soft rush on Mynd
> could be Bat for Lashes from the headphones
> placed on the dressing-table whispering
> Laura through light turning me apricot
>
> the ache of the wire in the wind returns
> to absent senders who are unaware
> of this flight tonight towards a few lines
> that still swarm with viral cultivation
>
> the water in the mill-stream winks & leaves
> together with the names of months & breeze
> as the creaky wheel continues to turn
>
> a simple tune will rearrange your brain
> remaining as a context for the news
> which still never speaks about our story

The text is rich in euphonious effects (affects). Soft, luscious vowel sounds, cluster Keatsian: soft rush … Lashes … phones … whispering … Laura through … turning me apricot … ache of the wire in the wind … the water in the mill-stream winks & leaves / together with the names of months & breeze; and pararhymes augment this: headphones / returns … Laura / through … cultivation / turn … leaves / breeze. There's a lullaby-ing here … except the poem is an aubade.

"…the soft rush on Mynd" refers to Long Mynd in the Shropshire Hills, perhaps an unusually idyllic (in the sense of Pastoral) setting within Hughes's Petrarchs (so far), where the settings are often abruptly, satirically, at odds with themselves. Interesting is the ear-kiss of synaesthesia here: as though the dawn moving over Long Mynd makes a soft, rushing, wind-like sound (or the sound of the wind rushing through rushes?).[22] This is then perhaps undercut or maybe augmented by the sound of pop music coming from a set of headphones left on "the dressing-room table." (Bat for Lashes is the stage name of Natasha Khan, a singer / instrumentalist; the lead single from her third album, *The Haunted Man*, is titled 'Laura').[23] It's a bedroom, the possible site of an erotic encounter, but the headphones whisper in a kind of (de)personification. Laura (?) is their absent wearer,

---

[22] "There is actually a plant covering the hills called 'soft rush'," Peter Hughes by e-mail.
[23] http://en.wikipedia.org/wiki/Bat_for_Lashes

but they also whisper her name "Laura" (suggesting to me Douglas Oliver's *Whisper "Louise"*).[24] And the "soft rush," beautiful as it is as a sonic representation of a visual phenomenon, suggests something working against the construction of an idyll (an idyll predicated upon a certain Ideal absence?), perhaps the rush of a drug fix or of a sugar rush. The music that whispers "Laura" from Laura's (?) headphones is maybe kitsch? but, again, is kitsch any sort of secure category, or does it metamorphose according to context? Is this a lullabying back to sleep at dawn?

Notice, too (allowing Petrarch back in for a moment) that in his sonnets Petrarch puns on Laura and l'aura, the Italian for breath or breeze. And in Petrarch's ms. text laura is written with no diacritical mark.[25] So the dawn over Mynd rushingly whispers, the headphones whisper—what? Laura's name? Or "Laura through light," a Neoplatonic stainless (dis)embodying?

My point is that there are so many complicities as well as complexities developing here. Literary criticism finds complexities to its taste, but complicities challenge cultural assignation and certification. The headphones abandoned keep on playing, and that registers the ubiquity of music that never seems to cease, that has no time for silence, that is always in your head, the music of mass entertainment—like you can't get thoughts of her or him out of your head. Yet / therefore it's also a wo(u)nder like love is(n't), whispering Laura in light. Not **ambiguity**; rather the outside / inside incessantly revolving of culture and culture industry replication / replacement (recall Walter Benjamin on the abandonment of the aura of the unique, the impossible to replicate. Or Laura's aura).[26] And yet, yet again, this is a dawn scene not the fall of some cultural / political night.

> the ache of the wire in the wind returns
> to absent senders who are unaware
> of this flight tonight towards a few lines
> that still swarm with viral cultivation

---

[24] Reality Street Editions, 2005.
[25] "Because Petrarch did not use the diacritical mark we call the apostrophe, Laura's name and the word l'aura (breeze, breath) are written by him in the same fashion. To the degree his collection is a love story, then, it is quite literally a love story about the evanescent and the transient." Barolini, op. cit. p. 38. Barolini is drawing on Peter Hainsworth, *Petrarch the Poet: An Introduction to the "Rerum vulgarium fragmenta"*, Routledge, 1988, p.135.
[26] Walter Benjamin, 'The Work of Art in the Age of Mechanical Reproduction' ('Das Kunstwerk im Zeitalter seiner technischen Reproduzierbarkeit'), first published 1936. http://www.marxists.org/reference/subject/philosophy/works/ge/benjamin.htm

The absence of the listener (recipient) to 'Laura' through headphones left on a bedside table now meets an uncanny double, or uncanny doubles (yet the reproducibility of the headphones' music makes it, too, indifferent as to the singularity of any listener). Now it's "absent senders," a strange reversal of the traditional situation of the Petrarchan lover, whose messages fall on closed ears, whose writings are met with averted eyes. "Ache," a human experience, or the ache or pangs of love / loss, are transmitted / transmuted to the transmitting "wire in the wind" and, again, human subject and mass produced object become unstable in their relations, metamorphose out and into one another's othernesses. And, yet yet yet again, those "few lines / that still swarm with viral cultivation"—do they signify hope (a resistance to sanitised and quiescent discourse, to authorised significations) or do they carry the threat of some sort of biological warfare (and its own fraternal double, terror and the terror of terror etc.)?

Speaking of incessantly revolving, "the creaky wheel continues to turn." This evokes song for me, or rather song-cycle: Schubert's *Die schöne Mullerin* (*The Lovely Maid of the Mill*). In Schubert's *Liederzyklus* a young man sets out to follow the course of a stream, wherever it takes him. He's a youthful version of that Romantic archetype, The Wanderer, and the stream takes him to a water-mill run by a jovial Miller with a beautiful daughter. The young man falls in love with the Miller's daughter and to his wonder she returns his affections. Then a huntsman clad in green arrives and the beautiful daughter falls in love with him, abandoning the youthful wanderer. In the final song, the stream or brook sings a lullaby to the young man ("Des Baches Wiegenlied"), a call to sleep in its "blauen kristallenen Kämmerlein," its blue crystal chamber, literally to go to bed upon its bed. Like Narcissus, the young man drowns in love's sorrow. Are we back in the same room as the dressing-room table and the headphones whispering 'Laura' / "Laura" through (crystal) light?

It seems like a moment of gentle, though melancholy, consolation and cultural conciliation. All is simple song, lullaby and aubade fold into one another's embrace, the headphones whisper on, the soft rush continues, the brook babbles its lullaby. But Schubert occurs elsewhere in Hughes's Petrarchs. Nothing is secure from banalisation, the depradations of power, the abuses of Capital and Fascism (Capital's uncanny / fraternal double):

> even nasty bastards have a soft side
> Mussolini collected toy meercats
> Michael Gove licks his snake to sleep each night
> George Bush whispered to bricks Pol Pot liked dogs

> Fascist eyelashes tremble to Schubert
> the lumps in their throats curtsey to the great
> graphic novels of the quattrocento
> & thick albino athletes made of rock

(From *Regulation Cascade*). Schubert becomes kitsch for murderers to emote to; quattrocento art receives their psychopathic approbation, and there are those whispers again, except it's not Laura whispering or Laura's name being whispered—except, it could be! The originator of the second great invasion of Iraq, the weapons of mass destruction liar, the neoliberal smash the poor "Crusader" with his cronies up to their eyeballs in oil money and lobbying interests—his wife's name is Laura.

Which leaves us, whoever us is, where? Hughes' Petrarch is a work in progress. It refuses to simplify situations in which the situated self finds itself, has times when that self despairs at the monumentality of an order of ordure stood against love without commerce, art without bourgeois recuperation (despairs of their possibility). But it starts again (the magic of the sonnet: a little room, once more, closed within its walls of 14 lines), with the memory of what it was and where it will be ghosting across times and places in its heads (like music through unworn headphones):

> is this art?
> I'm looking more than my age
> I'm strewn across my memory
> is this net shaping water?[27]

---

[27] Peter Hughes, from *Paul Klee's Diary*, section 2, in *Blueroads: Selected Poems*.

Riffingly
A right-read-through

Nigel Wheale

Wouldn't it be good to hire a skip, clear the decks, re-attempt a poetry of personal provision—an aspect of daily/local rites? Maybe not. But we're in Norfolk for most of the Summer & I hope to do a bit there.

I'm sitting down to tell myself why I really need this poetry, as if I didn't know.

Sometimes a small stream of silence runs through the matrices of the poem, which would have offended typographers of old, you may leap from bank to bank, or loiter at each side, there is no designated path, though the more you choose to take, the better, and right the way down, falling between the lines is also permitted:

breaks the fall of dawn	shock waves
on wrists & leaves	rumble through
a wild of nothing	tunnels ruptured
visible rind & pulp	pipes & voices

My Prince, your Jamesian ampersands, your tricksy hendiadys, how they foil our choices. And yet, finally, as clear as Roger, taking note from behind a hedge:

light around the edges

closer for another second

  glance to quick gold flick

this finch & zest of spring

There was a moment when the young Anglo poet looking for ways to (poetically) escape the island had to make that choice, just one of many:

to go off with Frank, and all the other guys who levelled with the street, or else tarry with Little JA in a Prospect of Flowers, a much more uncertain fate, I found at least. It's an "Are you a dog- or a cat-person issue", one feels. Peter strolled on, enjoying his own very particular *passeggiata*, usually with the dog in tow, and has been taking note, giving voice, ever since. And so he laid his lines down, or lifted them up, with the drawn bead of an old-time Mill Rd Shootist, negotiating his cruel yet flawless way through all the unknown poetistas who infested the sidewalk between the kebab shop and The Locomotive, in those days. I really like this, knew where I was then, if not to be found in that corner of The Six Bells, radically confused by *The Tennis Court Oath*.

Read the superb, quietly sustained diurnal of *The Summer of Agios Dimitrios* (2009), for instance; how many poets could so consistently maintain that interested, interesting focus on what just happens to be around—which doesn't preclude all sorts of excursions on the way. My particular favourite day is '4.5 Sunday 7th October', a short-lined aria that begins with galactic detail and resolves on "a fragment of bow … in a circle of ash / on the shingle / the only thing left / is her name". It is the steady pacing of attention through the line movement that is so pleasing, for this reader.

And then this journal powers up, takes on the longest elemental perspectives to meditate on all that rock, water, air, in the final section, 'Physical Geography'. 'Glaciation' makes a fine companion, even corrective, read to Jeremy Prynne's ice tendency, "The / moraine runs axial to the Finchley Road / including hippopotamus" [where] "a polar bear drives a white Princess". Both, for example, roam around "the Cromer ridge", for Jeremy, one of the "separable advances", for Peter, "what used to be bulges / now little pits & pingos", which is funnier. These elementals are where Peter Hughes comes closest to the playtime poetry of John Ashbery's *Rivers and Mountains*. He has picked up such lovely rocky words, all new to me, and I will place them on my poetical mantelpiece: clastic varves sustain the firn field. Isn't that really something, even if geologically meaningless?

And all that collaboration! Eeesh. It really worries me as to who stops where and who takes over, all that leaky wordage, the frantic baton changing, yet the sound of ten-ball tennis rings fluent above the net. What a performance, those riffs pinging between Brancaster and Valverde, mediated if not moderated by the Omniscient Mussel, D. Phil. Chub make their first appearance, unless I am very much mistaken, on page 104. As Cosimo said to the Queen's Peach, "it is hard to suck all the red words /

out of any local rock." I live in Orkney, and I should know. So just loosen up, for goodness' sake.

"I need to be a thousand miles south". We had a few drinks in the Geldart the evening before you both left for Italy, late September '83?, where as I remember you took a job translating manuals on decommissioning landmines, but with not very much Italian. Perfect preparation for the subsequent de-mining of language and perception, work of the true poet; Petrarca should be a push-over, just poke him with a very long stick. Italy enters the soul, via the tongue, as for so many of our friends, and stays there for ever, "my inner streets awash in the bright / burn of Ligurian wine". So that "the fine star fields around altair / in aquila" will always remain with us, and fire up the necessary courage to be able to look dauntlessly upon the comical yet sinister rubble through which we have to navigate, on our many days out in england & wales, all that "tod und verklärung farming today", on the way to the next campsite, where 'the warden is authorised to taser / autistic recipients of fuck-all'. You must try Scotland next, our clastic varves just have to be experienced, though in culinary terms we can't promise to match "the rogue gnocchi of Abergavenny".

I've ridden *The Metro Poems* so many times now, their perfection has become inescapable, sure lines rolling out down the stretch of the sonnet-tunnel. Their lovely compaction, which embraces so many constellations, asterisms, the detritus of Roman living, our poet perched upon a ledge, Lesbia's sparrow (who may have been a bullfinch). The assurance of the way that the metro ride is maintained, is flawless, a through-composed poem within which are so many pleasures for the taking. These poems know precisely what not to say. As your man Klee also knew, "After all, it's rather difficult to achieve the *exact* minimum, and it involves risks." And now, goodness, the TGV of the *Rime*, remorselessly one-way song to Laura, hotline from Brancaster *diretto* to all points south, plus everything in between across all six centuries. But what exactly is love this thing.

There *is* probably too much wine, both the red & the white, think of your periodontal well-being, my Dear, and all those dusk-to-dawn sessions will surely take their toll; poets of the new century tend to be in bed by 23:00 at the very latest, I know, I've met some. There are Workshops to be attended in the bright new morning, after all.

Nigel Wheale

Clare Short was granted a vision, immediately before she vanished. She saw all the youth of Handsworth staying home for the evening, just for a change, to sit alone in their bedrooms beneath the single naked light bulb, and read poetry. The streets became quiet, in a significant way. More of this kind of thing, please, Clare said, even two evenings a week, why stop there? Joy unto the youth of Handsworth, here are the pages to con o'er, far surpassing fretwork, truly much more than 'some unexceptional hobby'.

So on my read-thru everything, I've made such discoveries, revisited well-loved locales, generally on *Linea A* and environs. Will Self should check out *Site Guide*, he needs to get down and do some caravanning; 'Education Policy' should be nailed to Michael Gove's forehead, all right, just above his forehead; *Paul Klee's Diary* makes all kinds of new senses, must revisit München; *Minor Yours* is a rarely appropriate appropriation of our migrant suffering, and associated bestialisms. I did get a bit lost up *The Sardine Tree*, but will re-ascend, in search of bream. I promise to start listening to free-form musics, move on from Tavener of Boston, Lincs, and learn to love that horn. Also hire a skip, clear the decks, every day, plant fresh young rocks.

But just a thought about hedges; the heartfelt 'Education Policy' stipulates that all children must only "Write poetry about hedges", and it's right to say that poetry in school shouldn't be confined to the Nature Table in the corner. But then Roger in a sense never wrote about anything other than hedges, was rarely more ecstatic than when face-down in a hedgerow on the track of one of the rarer zygiella. And his explication of these lines could take you to the ends of the known universe,

> Once again I see
> These hedge-rows, hardly hedge-rows, little lines
> Of sportive wood run wild…

There are appropriate and inappropriate ways through this poetry. "the dog is my only philosopher / wagging its body & keeping its tail still", well OK, so there is to be no Heidegger in here, he sighed. Fair enough, no translucent sense of that which comes into being in all the lovely embodiments of this world, even now and as-such, via the word and only of these words? But what else may all this be, if not precisely that? There *are* too many dogs, though (we exempt Pegeen of blessed memory).

Nigel Wheale

I'm afraid I have to take the poet Rilke's view on this—who had in any case done everything that the philosopher of lederhosen aspired to, as the thinker himself ruefully avowed, *and* with rhythm—That the dogness of the dog is an *unendliche* and frankly unbearable appeal to we who should know better, having created this infinite dependency in the first place. He could not suffer them to be in the same room, he felt allergy in his very being, as-such, far beyond just sneezing. Woof. Try the Way of the Cat, I note almost no cats, other than the feral brutes of Agios Dimitrios. You like being feline, you know you do.

It's probably because of all the fish. What's with the fish? Thanks so much for the mullet, anyway.

Riff refs

All quotes from an exhilarated read-through: Epigraph, letter from Peter, 29 April 1999. 'breaks the fall', *Collected Letters* (2011), [2]; hendiadys: eg., 'But in the gross & scope of mine opinion', Horatio, *Hamlet*, 1.1.67 and note, Ann Thompson and Neil Taylor (eds), Arden (2006), citing George T. Wright, 'Hendiadys and *Hamlet*', *Proceedings of the Modern Language Association* 96 (1981), pp.168–93; 'as clear as Roger': 'few notice the corner bush / is already an airy cage / where small birds flip / almost silently', R. F. Langley, '*Matthew Glover*', *Collected Poems* (Carcanet/ infernal methods, (2000), p.30; 'a fragment of bow', *The Summer of Agios Dimitrios* (2009), p.34; 'The / moraine runs axial', J.H. Prynne, '*The Glacial Question, Unsolved*', *The White Stones* (1969), p.37; 'a polar bear', Peter Hughes, '*Glaciation*', *The Summer of Agios Dimitrios* (2009), p.79; 'light around the edges', ibid., [27]; 'ten-ball tennis', Peter Riley and John James, *Ten-ball Tennis: A Demonstration Match* (1970); chub, Peter Hughes and Simon Marsh, *The Pistol Tree Poems* (2011), p.104, Omniscient Mussel, passim; 'it is hard to suck', Peter Hughes and Gene Tanta, *Cosimo & The Queen's Peach* (2010), 8., p.12; 'I need to be a thousand miles south', 'my inner streets awash', *Paul Klee's Diary* (1995), pp.11, 13; 'the fine star fields', 'the warden is authorised', *Site Guide* (2011), Site 4, Site 8; 'tod und verklarung farming today', '*The Radio Sonnets*' 20, *Nistanimera* (2007), p.81; 'the rogue gnocchi', *Lynn Deeps* (MMX), 6; 'After all', Klee, *Diary*; 'some unexceptional hobby', *Paul Klee's Diary*, p.10; 'Education Policy', *Blueroads* (2003), p.61; 'Once again I see', William Wordsworth, '*Lines Composed a Few Miles above Tintern Abbey, on Revisiting the Banks of the Wye during a Tour. July 13, 1798'*, lines 14–6; 'the dog is my only philosopher', *Minor Yours* (2006), p.9.

See also Peter Riley's account of the generous eclecticism of Oystercatcher Press: http://fortnightlyreview.co.uk/2012/05/hughes-oystercatcher-press/

Oystercatcher Press

Ian McMillan

Just to say, I approach everything as an enthusiast rather than an expert. Read on!

I'm holding a bundle of Oystercatcher Press pamphlets in my hand; I grabbed them at random from a yard or so of Oystercatchers on my second shelf upstairs. I confess that I didn't know a great deal about Oystercatcher before I was a judge on the Michael Marks Pamphlet Award in 2010, but as soon as I saw them and read them I know they were the real thing. They feel like pamphlets rather than small books and they always add up to much more than the sum of their often tiny parts. Some of them are only a few pages long but they can sustain me on long train journeys or summer afternoons that fall into evenings.

Peter Hughes has said of Oystercatcher that he's not following any agenda, that he likes to approach the press in a sense of pluralism and excitement, and that's certainly the case. I'm going to open the bundle of Oystercatchers and spread them out on the table and listen to what they might tell me.

Luckily, the first one (and it really was at random, because I reckon Peter likes random) is by Peter Hughes himself, and it's called *Regulation Cascade*. They're versions of some of Petrarch's sonnets and within them I can feel my way into Peter's poetics. In the first one Peter/Petrarch writes "I invoke the idea of a poem as/perpetual enactment of pursuit…" Maybe I'll leave this pamphlet for a while and come back to it.

The next one on the table is one of my favourites, *Throe*, by Lisa Samuels; Lisa is an American poet who likes to play with language, and Ian Seed, in a review of *Throe*, noted her "ironic, self-effacing mockery" and a line like "oh baby you aren't here so you can't be alive" again seems to nail something about the Oystercatcher style. Something to do with being here, now. As Samuels says in a later poem "danger is a freedom to respond." Especially in Old Hunstanton.

MY Atrocity by David Kennedy tells us another Oystercatcher truth. In a note at the back of the pamphlet Kennedy writes that 'MY Atrocity' grew out of a triple reading; Roger Luckhurst's *The Trauma Question* (Routledge 2008) Alice Notley's *In the Pines* (Penguin 2007) and Keston

Sutherland's *Antifreeze* (Barque 2002) and this underlines the fact that Oystercatchers wear their learning lightly, that to make the most of these flocks of Oystercatchers you must read and read and read. This is true of all poetry, of course, but we're often seduced by deceptive slimness into thinking that it's going to be easy. "Hard, but worth it" is the tattoo you find somewhere on any Oystercatcher book. There's anger in Kennedy's book: anger and style: "scabby candle ruins the long table/in the courtyard of the old abbatoir/another sruck hour/struck in all my pipes tripes/sacs expandable bags…"

Lucy Sheerman's *Rarified (falling without landing)* tells me something else about Oystercatcher: these pamphlets can often be about beauty. They always look beautiful but they often contain great beauty too, like this: "She strolls over the small, bright square of grass,/each blade frosted with light, waxed lyrical./The real world creaking at the edge of sight." Sheerman can write in an intensely visual way, and I think Peter Hughes chooses his Oystercatcher poets with his eye as well as his ear and his heart.

Patterns feature heavily in a number of Oystercatcher pamphlets; patterns and lists and games. Richard Moorhead's *The Reluctant Vegetarian* is a twisting and turning surreal sequence of definitions of vegetables: here's the courgette: "n(1) peeled, hairless/dachshund pup on marble;/(2) green truncheon or glass spectrum; adj (3) thick/as a post box/gape;(4) heavy/as the stripped/and public smile/of someone/wronged". The late (and neglected) Anna Mendelssohn, in her pamphlet *py* gives us a series of deceptively simple acrostic poems built around the word "poetry": "photographs of snow/on mountains/explain our suffocation/tugged hard/reflecting identification/yarn strapped into fluorescent jackets". "prisoners-of-war/only an unending one/erudite in legalities/torn democrats swilled into sewage/reeks the hypocrisy of use/you who froze them melted then froze". As ever, the patterning and the list making take the reader to Oystercatcherish places, to an appreciation of the endless possibilities of languages simpler components, like the acrostic and the dictionary; it seems to me that part of Peter Hughes' mission with Oystercatcher is an unlocking one.

One of the great listmakers, shapemakers and patternmakers is Alec Finlay, and he's represented in my Oystercatcher bundle by *says you,* a collection not of lists or patterns but of some of Finlay's trademark tiny, shiny, gnomic utterances, this time dedicated to people and, to a lesser extent, places. "She writes me/a long letter//just to say/*I missed her ring.*" "She says/*listen to the wind*//I say/ *it's the wind.*" Finlay (and, by extension,

Hughes and Oystercatcher) take delight in the shifting of "ordinary" language into "extraordinary" language often by simply placing it on the page. Finlay celebrates the odd locutions of football commentators in a way that's full of love rather than contempt: "Steve Stone says/*the winger's// running round like/he's broken his leg.*" "Steve Claridge says/*this fellow// Alberto Riera's/the full McCoy.*"

Ian Seed's translations of the Italian poet Ivano Fermini in *the straw which comes apart* emphasise the internationalist edge to a lot of Oystercatcher's output. The press doesn't do a great deal of translations but the eyes and the ears of the Oystercatcher are always pointing across the water from Norfolk. English language poets can learn such a lot from poems like these, in Seed's sensitive versions: "on the horizon not even/was I mute but you held the pearls/and they gather around a thunderclap/the small eagle will carry the rags/sea/I haven't added up the waves/only fire with eyes the headstones/passing among men/the tears with a great rise and fall". As Seed writes, "Fermini's poems refuse any clear resolution or easy definition" and again that could be an emblem for some of Oystercatcher's output, and one of the exciting things about the press and Peter Hughes' stewardship of it is that you move from Alec Finlay's tiny and welcoming pieces to these gnarled and excitingly baffling lines. This Oystercatcher has a huge and voracious beak!

Sometimes the joy of opening an Oystercatcher Press jiffy bag is tied up with the excitement of encountering a writer you've not read before. Jessica Pujol i Duran is one such, and her collection *every bit of light* introduced me to the work of a young Catalan poet that I might not otherwise have come across. Her work is challenging, observant and full of a kind of music that seems, intriguingly and stimulatingly, to be slightly off-key: "like a Futurist attack urging me to change/my hair style. Then nothing, nothing,/flashes copying blackness, a race car./The only way out of here is to shake it:/ pat the cover, the body, kick the shelves,/crack it open and throw the jam away;/ then witness how it will be able to copy//the same all over again"

In the end, I think that Oystercatcher, with its catholic and eclectic list, is a mirror for Peter Hughes. Long may it thrive, long may he thrive through it.

Publishing Peter Hughes

John Welch

On the internet the other day, looking for a publisher for a pamphlet collection of English versions of an Iraqi poet I had been working with, I was struck by the barriers presses find it necessary to put up against the onslaught of poets brandishing their works. Overall, a majority of sites said "no unsolicited submissions". Others said they would only read manuscripts one month in the year. One publisher required you to download and fill in a long and detailed form before telling you whether or not you would be *allowed* to submit work. Maybe there was less pressure on poetry publishers back in 1975 when I set up The Many Press? It's true that a majority of the poets I published were people whose work I was already acquainted with, but Peter Hughes was one of the notable exceptions. It was in July 1982 that I received a letter with some poems: "Dear Mr Welch, Nigel Wheale… has suggested I send some of my poems…" Nigel was teaching at what was then Cambridge College of Arts and Technology, now Anglia Polytechnic University. *Bruised Light* was the suggested title.

The poems appeared in 1983, under the title *The Interior Designer's Late Morning*. It was his first publication. There was a particular firmness about the the writing, at times perhaps somewhat stilted, with scrupulous description often linked to place—the south coast, the Scilly Isles, France—and at the same time something stranger, as in the enigmatic narrative of the title poem. There is already that sense of the very near and the very distant referred to in the interview (see pages 13-23 of this volume) where he says: "I've always found—and this may go back to Hardy as well—that juxtaposition of the very small and transient with the biggest possible, and the way those things move against each other, stirring." As in 'Song':

> Our last night here and we claim the
> rhythms of the candle's moving light
> bringing the wind and that empty
> silent star at the centre of the sky
> together. About the old round table
> between us with its scraps of paper, timetables,
> finished bottle and two full glasses.

Bar Magenta appeared from The Many Press in 1988. It consisted of poems by Peter Hughes and Simon Marsh, prefiguring the directly collaborative work they were to do later in *The Pistol Tree Poems*. Simon Marsh is a musician and Bar Magenta, in Milan, is where the poets used to meet and The Many Press was to publish Marsh's *The Vinyl Hat Years* in 1995. Hughes' writing is here significantly freer and more relaxed. A lot of the poems are set in Rome. He had gone there as a teacher of "English as a Foreign Language" and describes Rome as an exciting experience: "being in a new environment in a new country, and behaving in a new language, I found very liberating." Going to Rome has traditionally had a momentous quality. Goethe's *Roman Elegies* celebrate his going there as a time of sexual fulfilment, while Sigmund Freud longed to go there, comparing Rome, with its layers going down and down, to the human psyche. It was a longing expressed in a series of dreams, but for a long time he couldn't get there—he would even set out for the city but find himself lingering in the Campagna unable to overcome his "Rome phobia". He finally made it in 1901.

Travel and tourism raise puzzling questions about what it means to be truly "there". The expatriate TEFL poet calls to mind Bernard Spencer, whose work has recently come back into focus with a new *Collected* edited by Peter Robinson (Bloodaxe 2011), as well as a collection of essays published by Shearsman. Spencer was perhaps the first such? Typically it's something that suggests sharply-focussed glimpses from an outsider. Spencer was to spend an entire teaching career working overseas, moving quite frequently; he was in Greece, Spain, Turkey, Italy, Cairo, Austria before his untimely and mysterious death in Vienna. It is in some ways a difficult position to sustain and In 'Letter Home', written in Madrid, he expresses a piercing sense of angst:

City where I live, not home, road that flowers with police,
what in all worlds am I doing here?

Peter Hughes' *The Metro Poems* express one person's particular way of being there. He of course was eventually to return to the UK where he embarked on a new teaching career, doing a PGCE and then working as a schoolteacher in primary schools, becoming in due course a deputy head.

I stayed in Rome with Peter on two occasions, for a week each time, in February 1989 and at Easter 1991. His flat at that time was in a modern block a short walk from Anagnina, the final station at one end of the Metro—the Rome Metro consisted of just two lines that crossed over one another—and in 1992 *The Metro Poems* appeared from The Many Press. Rome was an immensely powerful experience for me. *My* Rome was very much a matter of churches, monuments, and ruins. His on the face of it is very different. Not many churches or ruins except in oblique references. But at the same time a poem for *every* station on the Metro does imply a kind of comprehensiveness. Peter Hughes says of these poems that they "hovered around a sonnet shape" and it's as if this hinted-at structure holds Rome in a shadowy embrace, offering the possibility that all the diverse bits and pieces of the city might be swept up into this one container.

'Ottaviano', the opening poem, starts undersea and moves by degrees inland, to the shore "to where tangy spit dances on a reed" and then, in the last two lines, into the city itself:

> Town is a plane tree singing in the night wind
> Shadowing the steps to the underground.

Rome is a relatively small city, and its surroundings are frequently evoked as poems keep swooping or lurching into the surrounding landscape. In 'Repubblica':

> When the talk turns to baptism, I see the child
> a thousand feet higher—a river flowing through
> burnished ironstone pebbles and steep forest.
> The River Sangro, twenty five paces wide,
> shallow as water poured over the hands
> where they say wolves still come to drink at night.

Bits of urban nature are more likely to be referred to than monuments—the "elasticated emerald" of a lizard, "yellow weeds" growing beside the line "Fleetingly rocking, the dozy toddlers" as the train passes.

Back in the Eternal City Hughes' strategy could be described as "immersive", an expression currently used, it has to be said, with particular reference to TV documentaries where the presenter / protagonist is required to take part in the action, not comment from the sidelines. It's certainly not an expatriate's wary considered gaze. There's lots of clutter, lots of stuff. In 'Termini' there's a "lethargic rummage in the storeroom":

> Dusty unpaired shoes, *Catholicism Today,*
> The cardboard box the fridge came in…

> A ten-gallon Kilner jar of pickling vinegar
> Is crammed with a range of the country's pale
> Tasteless regrets, pressing at the glass…

"Erosive", "spatter", "curdling"—these are some of the are words that recur. There are rotting vegetables, "night smells of decaying courgettes". A good deal of word play for its own sake:

> Costermonger of dwarf and durous crabls
> Runt of sow and pimples' curds.

It's what the head is stuffed with, like the muddle in the cellar, a jumble of sense impressions, and it all gets shaken about before settling.

In 'S. Giovanni' the strategy of the writing of these poems is compared to fresco. The technique of fresco involves speed—the paint must be applied before the plaster finishes drying, so that paint and plaster can bond together. Leonardo famously thought he'd solved the problem of having to work quickly, when painting his 'Last Supper', by using paints of his own devising. It didn't work and quite soon chunks of it started to fall off. The poem opens:

> The theft of the next breath out of the air
> seems tricky and precipitous, each mouthful
> tasting of panicky evacuation

There's a sense of speed, and the perilous nature of improvisation, as the poem moves across the city, "traffic extended beyond every sense / to a dark incantation of night rain." Then the whole thing comes to rest as:

> A last watcher, clairaudient and delayed,
> traced the interwoven forms on the wall
> standing up to her neck in shadow.
> Evening light was saying the art is
> also to work fast on drying plaster.

Nigel Wheale refers, in a recent review in *Tears in the Fence* of Hughes' *Collected Letters* (Wild Honey Press 2011) to the poet's "lyric and sardonic gift". In sardonic vein traditional Rome edges its way in. In 'S. Paolo':

> The city is brimming with holy water,
> Swimmers are covered with rashes and boils.
> Every week the noise is heard of souls
> Being beaten into dust and incense.

The "rashes and boils", if I remember correctly, refer to swimming expeditions to Lake Nemi, a site charged with mythological significance but whose water was heavily polluted with fertiliser run-off from surrounding terraced fields. The dog was particularly badly affected.

The body and its all-encompassing sensations is central; in 'Giulio Agricola' it's the "Mind stuck on the sharp stick of the spine", suggesting those medieval images of an outstretched body encompassing the world and the stars. In 'Laurentina' the "raw blare of Arcturus" is "intimate and alien / as a stomach ulcer or disused urban canal". There's the sense of a body pushing along feeling its way through language. In 'Magliano':

> Craning up to the wobbling light I periscoped
> a finger to wiggle a feel of the sun.
> Dripping up the other bank, shedding weed and gudgeon
> I held the melted night tightly aloft—
> O how she'd plucked, revolved, doused down
> and scoured the gristly cockles of my heart.

These sensations are amplified from time to time by alcohol. In 'Arco di Travertino' "Quicksand chairs and dubbin wine yawn blasphemously". In 'Cinecittà' as she "popped the year's first peas from the pod" she:

> Poured chilled Torbato into the glasses
> That wink and sweat in the old Roman sun.

Sky and stars are repeatedly referred to. In 'Ponte Lungo':

> The path crosses a stream whose icy clarity
> plucks dregs spiralling into the lake
> like words dancing into oblivion.
> For a moment, from this angle
> the waters grow luminous. Another step
> and constellations sway by your feet.

And when the sequence ends, in 'Laurentina', the poem appears with a translation by the Italian poet, and friend, Riccardo Duranti (some of whose English language poems The Many Press was to publish in 1993 in *The Archer's Parado*x). It's a dawn epiphany, a moment of contained stillness where:

> Among cool, unheard movements of dark gardens
> first apple blossom is as still as the night

until:

> Top branches move in a breath of sunrise
> spilling petals, signalling another
> human dawn paling into significance.

Here the distance between "the very small and transient" and "the biggest possible" becomes momentarily resolved in "the sky's insubstantial consonance". In the interview referred to above he says, recalling childhood camping expeditions, "I look back at some poems of mine and think 'that's a religious poem for atheists'. Billowing awe and wonder on a cosmic scale held down by a few plastic tent-pegs. Reminds me of Doug Oliver's comment in 'An Island that is all the World': 'what does it mean to talk of spirituality in poetry when no religious belief lies behind the enquiry?'" Everyday muddle and clutter, the improvisational and verbally experimental, yielding poems that are humane, humorous and accessible, and not excluding the possibility of unclouded lyric utterance—it's an unusual and very enlivening combination.

Lightning Source UK Ltd.
Milton Keynes UK
UKHW04f1215270918
329545UK00001B/78/P

9 781848 612969